WATERSIDE WALKS
In Norfolk

Geoff Pratt

COUNTRYSIDE BOOKS
NEWBURY, BERKSHIRE

First published 2000
© Geoff Pratt 2000

COUNTRYSIDE BOOKS
3 Catherine Road
Newbury, Berkshire

To view our complete range of books,
please visit us at
www.countrysidebooks.co.uk

ISBN 1 85306 621 4

Designed by Graham Whiteman
Cover illustration by Colin Doggett
Photographs and maps by the author

Produced through MRM Associates Ltd., Reading
Printed by Woolnough Bookbinding Ltd., Irthlingborough

Contents

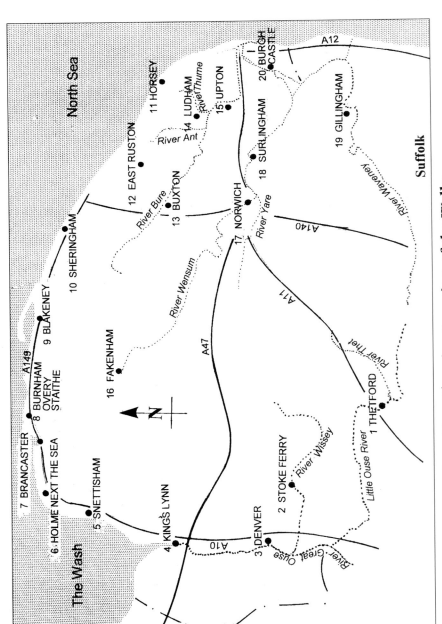

Area Map Showing Location of the Walks

Walk

In memory of my sister-in-law, Mary Eileen Bird who helped research this book

Publisher's Note

We hope that you obtain considerable enjoyment from this book; great care has been taken in its preparation. Although at the time of publication all routes followed public rights of way or permitted paths, diversion orders can be made and permissions withdrawn.

We cannot, of course, be held responsible for such diversion orders and any inaccuracies in the text which result from these or any other changes to the routes nor any damage which might result from walkers trespassing on private property. We are anxious though that all details covering the walks are kept up to date and would therefore welcome information from readers which would be relevant to future editions.

INTRODUCTION

What better place could there be to enjoy a waterside walk than the county of Norfolk! There is truly something here for everyone, from exhilarating coastal paths to rural river retreats, not to mention the wonderful expanse of the Broads.

Norfolk is practically surrounded by water. It has the North Sea on two sides and the River Great Ouse is close to its western boundary. On the southern side, the county boundary follows the River Waveney and the River Little Ouse. Both these rivers have their source in Redgrave and Lopham Fen, an area of marshland. Many people have their first glimpse of waterway life on the Broads where an extensive network of navigable waterways connects the rivers Waveney, Yare and Bure, their tributaries and the broads from which the area derives its name.

The 20 circular walks described in this book are between 2 and 7 miles long and they all include walking beside flowing water, or the sea. Most of the paths are well waymarked and none should prove difficult to use.

Many people seek refreshment after, or during, their walk. There are usually several options available but I have briefly described, for each walk, a pub, restaurant or café within a reasonable distance, which I have used and found pleasant.

I have drawn sketch maps, not to scale. Numbers on the map refer to paragraph numbers in the text. It is always a good idea to have the relevant Ordnance Survey map with you as well and the appropriate map numbers are given in the walk directions.

A parking place, or places, has been described for each walk. However at the peak of the season, parking places can fill very quickly particularly in the Broads area and on the Norfolk coast. Care should be taken when parking, not to cause an obstruction. Modern agricultural machinery can be very wide!

I would like to thank my family for their encouragement and help and also thank friends Dick Leech and Joan Picton who joined me in research trips in Norfolk, and Len and Beryl Watkins who, beside accompanying me on several trips, provided invaluable information about Norwich.

I hope you get great enjoyment from exploring some of Norfolk's beautiful watery byways!

Geoff Pratt

TWO RIVERS AT THETFORD

❧❀❧

Two rivers – the Little Ouse and the Thet – enhance this delightful walk that begins at the heart of the historic market town of Thetford. Walk upstream to the Nuns Bridges and a tranquil nature reserve, then explore the old streets below the Castle Hill. This riverside walk is the very best way of taking in some of Thetford's dramatic past.

The Nuns Bridge

Thetford is a thriving market town, close to the southern edge of Norfolk and at the confluence of the Little Ouse with its tributary, the River Thet. Here the ancient Icknield Way crossed the rivers and an important settlement grew up. There was an Iron Age fort here, and much later a Norman castle – until Hugh Bigod, Norman master of East Anglia – turned traitor and his castle was destroyed by Henry II. An earlier Bigod, Roger, had founded the priory. Once it, like the castle, would have dominated the town.

Alongside the Town Bridge, at the start of the walk, is the Anchor

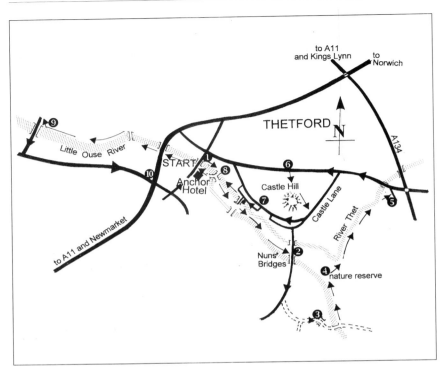

Hotel. In the pleasant bar, situated close to the river, you can choose from a variety of snacks including jacket potatoes with a wide choice of fillings, or more substantial meals from their menu. Telephone: 01842 763925.

- **HOW TO GET THERE:** Follow the A11 Thetford bypass to the roundabout at the B1107 and A134 intersection. Take the A134 towards Bury St Edmunds. In about ¾ mile, at the traffic signals cross straight over and then turn left along Bridge Street, Town Bridge is just along the road.
- **PARKING:** A convenient car park is beside the river just to the west of Town Bridge, though there are several more car parks surrounding the pedestrianised streets comprising Thetford Town Centre. Follow the signs.
- **LENGTH OF THE WALK:** 4 miles, or a shorter walk of 2 miles. Maps: OS Landranger sheet 144 Thetford & Breckland; OS Pathfinder 943 Thetford (GR 869830).

THE WALK

1. From the Town Bridge follow the paved riverside walk and cross the green-painted three-way bridge on to Butten Island. A gravel path leads across the wooded island. Look left to see the mill. The path leads out to a narrow road. Turn right and very soon cross a wooden footbridge. Immediately after, leave the surfaced path, turning left along a grass footpath. Before long you are on a hard path again. After crossing an overflow watercourse beside sluice gates, take the broad path along the grassy banks of the Little Ouse River.

2. The footpath ends at a road beside the old narrow twin-arch brick bridge, which is paired with a bridge over the River Thet and known as the Nuns Bridge. This is probably where the ancient Icknield Way crossed the rivers. Turn right over the bridge and follow the road for about 275 yards. Turn left along Nunnery Place, passing several old buildings and eventually the former Benedictine convent, now offices of the British Trust for Ornithology (BTO). After passing Nightingale Way on the right keep straight on into a country lane between hedges. An information board explains that you are on a permissive path through a Nature Reserve owned and managed by the BTO.

3. Cross a cart bridge over a narrow watercourse and shortly cross the Little Ouse River. Immediately turn left on a narrow path along the riverbank with the river on the left.

4. Eventually, glimpsing Nuns Bridge again ahead, you will see another BTO information board. Here turn right along a footpath and soon, after crossing a slatted footbridge, enter a marshy wood. When you reach the bank of the River Thet, continue beside the winding river. Look out for an information board which will give you information about the birds and animals which inhabit this area.

5. Leaving the river, the path climbs steps to a road, Arlington Way. Turn left and in about 50 yards turn left again, cross the River Thet, and pass The Bridge pub. Walk along the road towards Thetford, with Melford Common on the right. Pass Castle Lane off to the left.

6. At the far end of Castle Meadow go left along a surfaced footpath which leads down through the Iron Age ramparts to pass Castle Hill, and the remains of the Norman motte and bailey, on the right. Beyond the castle turn right along the road to walk through the old part of the town. Green Heritage plaques mark the buildings of interest in this historic town.

7. Pass Ford Place on the left and bear right into Old Market Street. Notice the Old Gaol, on the left, just before Ford Street. Turn left along Nether Row, and follow it round to the right. Take the next turning left to the River Thet and the Old Mill. Turn right beside the river and follow it back to the three-way bridge you crossed earlier.

8. Cross to the car park and continue beside the river to the Town Bridge. You are back at the start and could end the walk here.

To complete the whole of the walk, cross straight over Bridge Street and take the riverside path downstream. Go under a road bridge and before long turn right to cross the river on Blaydon Bridge. Keep beside the river on your left.

9. After passing a flood control weir swing right along a surfaced footpath up to a road, Canterbury Way. Go left and recross the river. Swing left on a surfaced footpath and turn left at the main road (A134). Before long pass Canons Close on the left and then there is a wide triangular green. Find a narrow path leading from the green to the ruined Norman chapel of the Canons of the Holy Sepulchre. This 12th century flint-walled building is an English Heritage site and is open, free of charge, at most reasonable hours. An information board within the walls will tell you its history.

10. Retrace your steps to the road. At the traffic signals go straight on. In about 275 yards turn left along Bridge Street. Pass the old Grammar School and return to the Town Bridge and the start.

PLACES OF INTEREST NEARBY

The *Burrell Museum* in Minstergate commemorates the area's industrial past. Burrell steam traction engines and farm machinery were made here. Open April to October on Saturdays, Sundays and Bank Holiday Mondays. Telephone: 01842 752599. Just off the A134, 7 miles north of the town, is *Grimes Graves*. At this English Heritage site, you can descend into an excavated Neolithic flint mine 4,000 years old, where early man dug the material with which to fashion tools and weapons. Open daily April to October. Telephone: 01842 810656.

THE RIVER WISSEY AT STOKE FERRY

᠂᠀᠂

From Stoke Ferry this peaceful walk follows the willow-clad bank of the River Wissey. Passing a set of large sluice gates that control the flow of water, there is a short diversion to see an aqueduct where the river crosses over the Cut-off Channel. Returning to the sluices, the route continues along a grassy and wooded bank beside the placid waters of the Channel.

The Cut-off Channel

Almost at the edge of the Fens, the village of Stoke Ferry lies on the River Wissey, a tributary of the Great Ouse. Stoke Ferry was an important little river port and trading centre in days past, when the lighters tied up at the staithe. Close by, the Cut-off Channel was dug in the 1950s to relieve flooding in the Fens, running along a contour and discharging to the River Great Ouse, dowstream. Here you will see that it runs under the Wissey, and in times of flood this river – and the Little Ouse and the Lark – can be diverted direct into the Channel. You are

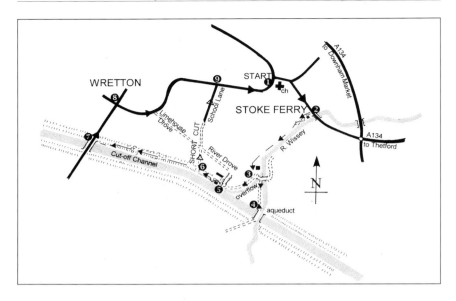

never far from the realisation of the danger of flood water in this low-lying and beautiful land.

The Woodland Lodge at the Comfort Inn is about 4 miles from Stoke Ferry, at Northwold on the A134 road. The spacious bar and the Forest Restaurant are in a building separate from the Hotel and Conference Centre. The menu offers a good range to suit all tastes. Several fish dishes, steaks, and a mixed grill including liver, sausage, gammon, steak, eggs and onion rings, is among the food served. A wide range of bar snacks is also available. Telephone: 01366 728888.

- **HOW TO GET THERE:** Stoke Ferry is about 15 miles south of King's Lynn, on the A134 road to Thetford. The main road bypasses Stoke Ferry so leave the A134 at the roundabout at the eastern end of the village.
- **PARKING:** There is a car park in the centre of the village by the west end of the church.
- **LENGTH OF THE WALK:** 4 miles; short cut 2 miles. Maps: OS Landranger sheet 143 Ely, Wisbech & surrounding area; OS Pathfinder 921 Southery & Methwold (GR 704999).

THE WALK

1. From the car park by the church, go to the road junction and turn right along the village street, passing the church on the right. Keep along the main road, which bends round to the right. Turn right about 20 yards before the bridge over the River Wissey.

2. Follow a signed bridleway beside a row of willows on the left. At first the path is quite narrow and after the trees it bends right and left around some bushes to come out to the riverbank. Walk beside the river on a grassy path. Before long you will see ahead, the massive top structure of two sluice gates. The path deviates a little from the riverbank, looping round a brick building to meet a gravel drive.

3. Just by the fence of Sluice No 2 find a narrow path, between fences, which leads across an overflow channel alongside the sluice gate. On the far side climb a few steps to a concrete road. Turn right to follow the River Wissey on the left.

4. In about 450 yards you will come to the Cut-off Channel and the aqueduct carrying the flow of the Wissey across it. Retrace your steps back to the sluice gate and recross the channel. In normal conditions you would expect the sluice to the main river to be open, and the sluice to the overflow channel to be closed.

On reaching the gravel track, turn left and walk parallel to the overflow channel. There is a reed-covered lake on the right. Cross a culvert over a drainage ditch in a deep ravine, and nearby you will see that the overflow channel has joined the Cut-off Channel.

A view down the Cut-off Channel

5. Keep straight on beside a tall fence enclosing the waterworks on the right. In just over 50 yards turn right in front of a brick pumping station. Turn left just before the waterworks gate, walking along a wide green sward between security fences. Soon return to the bank of the Cut-off Channel.

When you reach the corner of the fence on the right, swing right, as waymarked. Climb a grassy bank and continue along a broad path on top of the bank with a fine view of the straight wide watercourse receding into the distance. The slopes of the channel are lined with trees and shrubs, giving a very attractive appearance.

6. Pass on the right the end of a road. This is School Lane and provides a short cut back to the village. For the full walk, keep straight on along the bank, which was formed by the material excavated from the channel. The vegetation on the bank gradually increases and soon you are walking along a narrow footpath through woodland. Eventually the path swings left off the bank to a lower track.

7. On reaching a bridge over the channel, go out through a gate to a road, turn right and in about 550 yards reach a crossroads in Wretton.

8. Turn right towards Stoke Ferry along Wretton Fen Road. Keep along the road passing the end of Limehouse Drove and later pass Ivy Farm on the left.

9. Look out for School Lane (the end of the short cut) on the right. After passing the Community School on the right the road bends left back to the church, the car park and the start.

PLACES OF INTEREST NEARBY

Just 3 miles north-east lies *Oxborough Hall* (National Trust). A 15th century moated hall, its rooms are furnished in the styles of different periods. The gardens and woods are also open, and there is a restaurant for refreshments. Generally open April to October except Thursdays and Fridays. For details telephone 01366 328258. Cockley Cley is about 4 miles beyond Oxborough Hall. Near this village is a reconstruction of an *Iceni Settlement*, farm museum and nature reserve. For information telephone 01366 328258.

DENVER AND THE GREAT OUSE

Starting beside the massive sluice gates at Denver, this walk follows the bank of the River Great Ouse and then the Relief Channel to reach and explore the attractive old market town of Downham Market. The walk continues along a lane to Denver and later returns to the start passing the fine Denver Windmill, built in 1835.

The river, with Denver Sluices in the background

Originally, the Fens were just low-lying waterlogged marsh, but in 1631 Cornelius Veermuyden constructed a straight channel about 20 miles long, now called the Old Bedford River, that discharged into the River Great Ouse near the small village of Denver. Since those days much more drainage work has been done and now Denver is the terminal point of four great watercourses linking into the Great Ouse: the Old and the New Bedford Rivers, the Relief Channel and the Cut-off Channel. The flow of water is controlled by massive sluice gates.

Just beyond the sluice gates on the bank of the River Great Ouse

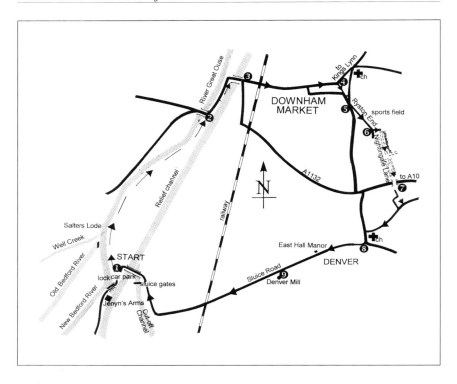

stands the popular Jenyns Arms. Here you may eat and drink in comfortable pleasant surroundings overlooking the river, and watch the boats sail past. The menu offers a full range of interesting and tasty meals. There is also a broad waterside terrace. Telephone: 01366 383366.

- **HOW TO GET THERE:** Denver is just over a mile south of Downham Market. If you follow the A10 Cambridge to King's Lynn road, at a T-junction just south of Downham Market go west along the A1122. Turn left at the first junction to Denver and at the church, where the main road makes a sharp bend, turn right along Sluice Road and continue for about 3 miles.
- **PARKING:** There is a large unsurfaced car park close to the Denver Sluice Gates. There are public toilets here.
- **LENGTH OF THE WALK:** 5½ miles. Maps: OS Landranger sheet 143 Ely, Wisbech & surrounding area; OS Pathfinder 900 Downham Market & Marham and 899 Wisbech (South) (GR 589011).

THE WALK

1. From the District Council car park go out to the road and turn left for about 50 yards rising up to the Denver Sluice Gates. Just before the road crosses the river, turn right through a small gate and follow the Fen Rivers Way along the bank of the River Great Ouse. The path lies along the top of a raised grassy bank that slopes down to the Great Ouse on the left and a broad low-lying meadow on the right.

In about 350 yards, on the opposite side of the river, pass the sluice gate where the Old Bedford River discharges and nearby a lock at Salters Lode where Well Creek, a continuation of the old course of the River Nene, joins the Great Ouse. Continue along the riverside path, there are a few gates and stiles to negotiate en route. Half right, in the distance you will see the town of Downham Market.

2. Cross a stile and reach a road at a bridge over the river. Join the road, which runs parallel to the river 50 yards away on the left. At the end of garage premises on the right, go right across a small park to the bank of the Relief Channel and turn left beside it. Continue to the road and turn right across Hythe Bridge.

Denver Mill

3. On the far side of the bridge, go straight on at the mini-roundabout and enter the historic market town of Downham Market. Cross a level crossing just by the railway station and keep straight on. Pass on the right Shelley Cottage, built in local brown carstone, and later keep straight on at the start of the traffic one-way system. You will come to a small town square. The Town Hall is on the right but most prominent is the Memorial Clock on an octagonal base, presented to the town by James Scott in 1878.

4. From the clock, turn right along High Street. In 100 yards or so, go straight on at the road junction at the end of the one-way system. Pass the post office on the right and come to a junction where an ornamental Town Sign stands on a grassy traffic island.

5. Just beyond the junction, cross London Road and bear left along Ryston End, a narrow road. Before long pass the Downham High School Sixth Form Centre, on the left. After the last building on the left there is an old stone boundary wall beyond which is the High School sports field. Look over the wall about 20 yards from the start, and you will see a small quaint building a few yards away. It has an ornamental door and no windows and may be the remains of an old icehouse.

6. On reaching the corner of the playing field, turn left. In 100 yards or so, turn right along Nightingale Lane, a gravel track, following a hedge on the right. At a junction of tracks keep straight on, still beside the hedge, and later walk along a narrow path between two rows of tall trees.

7. The path leads to a bridge over the main road and immediately after the bridge, the path joins the end of a cul-de-sac. In a few yards the road swings right, but keep straight on across a wide grassy area to reach a road about 100 yards away. Turn right into Denver.

8. At St Mary's church turn left. At the corner of the churchyard where the main road bends sharply left, keep straight on, carefully crossing the road, and walk along Sluice Road, passing the War Memorial on the left. Look out for a plaque on the wall of East Hall Manor, commemorating Captain George W. Manby FRS who invented a rocket life-saving apparatus for use in shipwrecks that has saved hundreds of lives since the early 1800s.

9. Soon see ahead, and later pass on the left, Denver Mill. Continue along the road and cross a level crossing. In about 500 yards the road bends right, and then shortly turns left to cross the Cut-off Channel. Look left to see the sluice gates upstream. Immediately after, cross the Relief Channel and follow the road round to the left back to the car park and the start.

PLACES OF INTEREST NEARBY

About 12 miles to the west is the interesting Cambridgeshire town of *Wisbech*. Here visit *Peckover House* (National Trust), a fine 18th century town house with gardens. Telephone: 01945 583463. By contrast, a similar distance to the east at Swaffham, is *Ecotech*, an exhibition about the history of the earth and life on earth. Open April to October. Telephone: 01760 726100.

THE GREAT OUSE AT KING'S LYNN

This fascinating walk explores King's Lynn's historic river frontage, and crosses the River Great Ouse by a ferry to the village of West Lynn. After walking upstream to the Free Bridge, you return along the quayside, passing the 17th century Custom House.

The waterfront at King's Lynn

The town of King's Lynn stands on the east bank of the River Great Ouse not far from where its waters discharge into the Wash. It is as a port that the town has become important, originally serving the waterborne traffic along the Great Ouse and its tributaries as well as the wool trade from East Anglia. Ranged behind the warehouses and the quay are many interesting old buildings, the homes of former merchants. The magnificent Custom House building is a monument to the importance of the trade that was generated here. The town has two ancient market squares – a Saturday Market and a Tuesday Market that

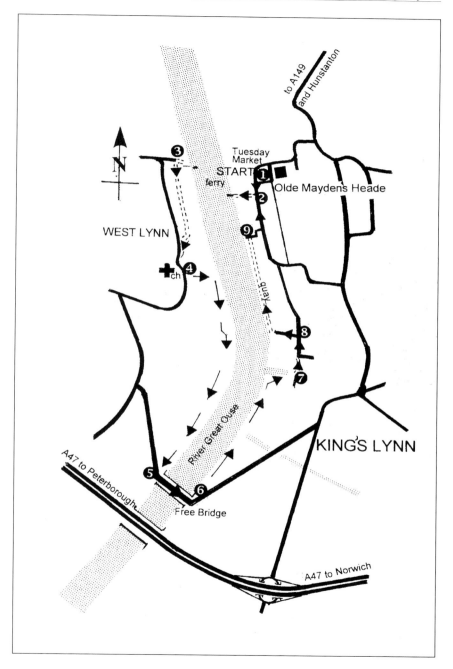

have been in use since the 12th century, and it is the business centre for a large part of West Norfolk.

Among the buildings facing the Tuesday Market Place is Ye Olde Mayden's Heade. This is a comfortable and popular pub offering a carvery with a variety of roast joints and also serving a choice of tasty pies, with shortcrust pastry. Telephone: 01553 774699. Not far away, at the King's Lynn Arts Centre, is the Crofters Coffee Shop below the theatre and the pleasant Riverside Restaurant, overlooking the River Great Ouse.

- **HOW TO GET THERE:** King's Lynn is served by the A10 road from Cambridge and the A47 from Norwich. The start of the walk is at the Tuesday Market, which is at the northern end of the main shopping streets.
- **PARKING:** The pedestrianised town centre is ringed with short term and long term car parks. There is parking in the Tuesday Market and also on the South Quay beside the river, just south of the Custom House.
- **LENGTH OF THE WALK:** 3 miles. Maps: OS Landranger sheet 132 North West Norfolk; OS Explorer 23 Norfolk Coast West (GR 616203).

THE WALK

1. Start at the Tuesday Market Place. Go to the south-west corner of the square and walk along Kings Street, passing the Globe Hotel on the right. Very soon pass 15th century St George's Guildhall, which is now the King's Lynn Arts Centre.

2. In a short distance turn right down narrow Ferry Lane, a pedestrian way leading to the river and the ferry landing stage. Take the ferry across the River Great Ouse to West Lynn. The ferry runs roughly every 20 minutes until 5.50 pm.

Arriving at the West Lynn landing stage, walk straight on, out to a road. A notice says that this point is the start of the Peter Scott Walk, a 10-mile trail along the remote coastline of the Wash.

3. Turn left along the road. Where the road bears right, keep straight on along a one-way street, soon swinging right to return to the road opposite the Swan public house. Bear left along the road.

4. Very soon, just as you come to a big lay-by opposite Cherry Tree Drive, climb the grass bank behind a concrete retaining wall and turn left along a grass path running on the top of a raised bank. On the right are the Lynn Bowls Club and a children's play area. Climb the 17 steps to the top of the flood protection bank and here you will see on the opposite side of the water, Lynn's South Quay and behind it, St Margaret's church. Over to the left you will see the Custom House. Continue along the broad grass path beside the tidal river. On the far bank, moored at the southern end of the quay you may see some fishing boats. You have left West Lynn behind you and at the foot of the flood bank on the right there is an arable field.

5. Eventually the riverside path reaches a road. Turn left and cross the Free Bridge. Upstream is a modern bridge which carries the A47 King's Lynn Bypass.

6. On the far side of the bridge turn left, along the top of a grassy bank similar to that on the other side of the river. The River Great Ouse is now on the left and King's Lynn is ahead. You have joined the Fen Rivers Way, a long distance path from Cambridge. Pass on the right the end of a drainage ditch. The path becomes a tarmac cycle track. Keep straight on along it and later the path loops right, round a small creek and soon reaches a road.

7. Turn left along the road and before long, go through a small arched gateway, and soon reach Bridge Street. Look out on the left for The Greenland Fishery, a 17th century half-timbered building, once a merchant's house and later a tavern serving the whale fishermen of the time – hence the name.

8. At the junction with Bridge Street turn left, following the sign to South Quay. On reaching the river turn right and walk along the Quay.

9. Just before the end of the Quay turn right for 100 yards or so, parallel to a small creek. Then turn left, soon to pass the Custom House, now the Information Bureau, and continue back along Kings Street to the Tuesday Market.

PLACES OF INTEREST NEARBY
About 5 miles north of King's Lynn stands *Castle Rising* (English Heritage). The castle comprises a massive Norman keep within a ramparted area. Telephone: 01553 631330.

SNETTISHAM AND THE WASH

You can enjoy bird watching and wide sea views on this exhilarating walk by the shores of the Wash. After following the shore line, the walk turns inland beside drainage ditches and across coastal pasture to the equally attractive landscape of a wooded hillside and Snettisham Common.

Snettisham Coastal Park

At high tides and in stormy weather North Sea waves can lash the shores of the Wash and this walk starts about 2 miles west of Snettisham village along the top of a shingle bank which protects the low-lying hinterland, giving wonderful views over sea and land. By contrast, the receding tides uncover large areas of mud flats and sandbanks, which attract numerous sea birds. The Wash is a nationally important Site of Special Scientific Interest and fringing the beach is the Snettisham Coastal Park, open for the public to enjoy. Visitors are also welcome to the RSPB Nature Reserve, not on this route but situated

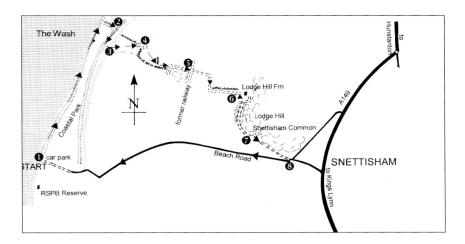

only a short walk southwards along the sea wall. There are four hides overlooking the reserve.

Just off the main village street in Snettisham, on a road leading towards the church, is the Rose and Crown. Dating from the 14th century, there is an old-world feel about the place. There are three bars and a restaurant. Beams in the ceiling are decorated with fascinating old tools. If the lay-by in front is full, there is a large car park, approached from a lane beside the inn. The menu offers a selection of interesting dishes, for example Brancaster Mussels in lemon and dill cream sauce, or roulade of pork and smoked salmon with prunes, carrot and swede, but look out for the 'specials' on the blackboard (pheasant was available when I was there). Telephone: 01485 541382.

- **HOW TO GET THERE:** From the Snettisham bypass on the A149 road between King's Lynn and Hunstanton, turn westward along Beach Road (signed Snettisham Beach), to the end of the road.
- **PARKING:** The walk starts at the beach car park situated at the end of Beach Road. There is a public toilet nearby.
- **LENGTH OF THE WALK:** 4 miles. Maps: OS Landranger sheet 132 North West Norfolk; OS Explorer 24 Norfolk Coast East (GR 648335).

THE WALK

1. From the car park climb the shingle bank overlooking the sea and walk northwards towards Hunstanton, along the broad gravel track on

A quiet spot by the park

the top of the bank. The beach slopes away to the left and the Coastal Park lies on the right.

Keeping to the top of the bank, pass a bird hide on the right of the track. About 400 yards beyond it, come to a point at the start of a long lake, parallel to the coast. Turn right, descending the bank and, passing the end of the lake on the left, climb another bank about 200 yards away.

2. On reaching the top, you will see a broad watercourse ahead of you. Note, on the left, a stile in the boundary fence of the Coastal Park; northwards from the stile, a public footpath continues along the bank to the next village of Heacham. But now, continuing the walk, turn right along the top of the bank beside the reed-fringed watercourse on the left. In about 200 yards look out for a kissing gate beside a farm gate seen beyond the water on the left. Take the path on a causeway between two sections of the broad ditch to reach the gate.

3. From the kissing gate, cross the meadow, at first going parallel to the fence on the right. Half way along the field bear slightly left, away from the fence which swings right. Leave the field through a gap and cross a culvert. Immediately after, turn right over another culvert, as signed, into the corner of the adjacent field.

4. Walk diagonally across the meadow to a gap at the far corner, and then continue parallel to a hedge on the right. At the next field corner cross a stile beside a steel gate and follow a sandy cart track with a wood on the right and a ditch on the left.

5. At the end of the wood cross, at right angles, a track along an old railway line. About 300 yards away on the right you may see a railway platelayers' hut, formerly used by a track maintenance gang. The sandy cart track becomes a hard gravel farm road. Straight ahead you can see Lodge Hill Farm behind which are the wooded slopes of a small hill. Follow the track which bends right and then left beside a hedge on the left. At a footpath sign about 150 yards before the farm, turn half right along a grassy headland path beside a fence on the left.

6. At the far side of the field turn right at the edge of a wood along a broad grass path with a row of mature trees on the right.

7. After passing through a steel gate beside a wooden farm gate, ignore a broad track branching left and walk straight on through Snettisham Common. Keep to the path, which after getting somewhat narrower comes out past a car park to the junction of Common Road and Beach Road.

8. Turn sharp right along Beach Road for about 1½ miles to return to the start at Snettisham Beach.

PLACES OF INTEREST NEARBY

Just 6 miles south of Snettisham is the royal residence of *Sandringham.* The house is open generally between April and October (except for a fortnight in July). The magnificent 60 acres of gardens and grounds are also open as is the museum, housing royal mementoes. Telephone: 01553 772675. A fragrant meadow garden, a gift shop and tea room can be visited at *The Norfolk Lavender Farm* at Heacham. Guided tours are available in the summer. Telephone: 01485 570384.

WALK 6

HOLME NEXT THE SEA

Looking out over the wide sweep of the sea, this lovely walk begins along the Norfolk Coast Path, then crosses sand dunes, parallel to the shore, and later skirts a Nature Reserve, following an inlet to the staithe at Thornham. Going through the village the walk climbs the sandy hill behind the coastal marsh and continues along the crest of the hill, returning to Holme along a part of the ancient Peddars Way.

Thornham Staithe

The Romans built a highway northwards to reach the sea at what is now Holme next the Sea. This road, which probably followed the route of an earlier track, was built on higher land, avoiding the swamps and marshes of the Great Ouse basin. The Peddars Way, as it is known today, is still in use, now as a National Trail linking to the Icknield Way at Knettishall Heath on the Norfolk boundary. This is an ancient land – on the shore here in 1998/9, a tide uncovered a circle of Bronze Age wooden posts, believed to have been a 'Woodhenge'. These relics have since been excavated and removed for preservation and will be displayed elsewhere.

The Lifeboat Inn in Ship Lane, Thornham, situated on the route, dates from the 16th century. Besides several bars, there is a pleasant glazed loggia at the rear and an ancient vine in a conservatory. The menu has a wide selection of fish dishes including oven-baked halibut. Other fare includes lambs liver and bacon, and pork medallions. Telephone: 01485 512236.

- **HOW TO GET THERE:** Off the A149 coast road, about 2 miles north-east of Hunstanton, take the junction signed 'Holme Beach ¾' and continue to the end of the road.
- **PARKING:** There is a large car park at Holme Beach. A public toilet is nearby.
- **LENGTH OF THE WALK:** 7 miles. Maps: OS Landranger sheet 132 North West Norfolk; OS Explorer 23 Norfolk Coast West (GR 697439).

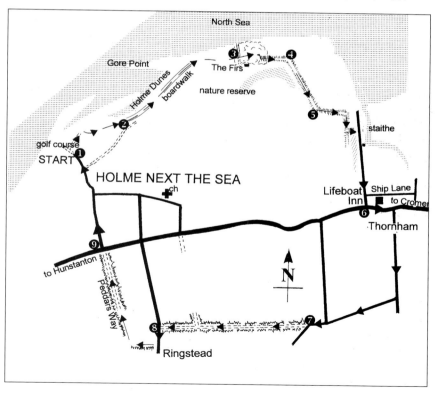

THE WALK

1. From the beach-side car park, go out to the road and turn right towards the shore. Cross part of the golf links – watch out for golfers! Go straight on past the iron gate. An acorn waymark indicates that this is part of the long distance Norfolk Coast Path. In about 50 yards swing right past a white notice describing the Holme Dunes Nature Reserve of the Norfolk Wildlife Trust. The path is a broad sandy track through typically coastal vegetation. Before long bear round to the right, as waymarked, climbing slightly and following a line of stakes fringing the golf course. Keep straight on. Over to the right, notice a curious observation tower.

Come to a timber walkway through the sand dunes and pass on the right a white chalet bungalow. A little later, immediately to the right at the foot of a bank, pass the Nature Reserve car park. Looking out over the wide sweep of the sea, the salt marsh in the foreground is called Lavender Marsh. The sandy spit is Gore Point.

2. Continue along the timber walkway. Soon after the car park you will see to the left several stumpy trees which have been moulded by the prevailing wind. Pass, on the left, a creek which heads out to sea at Gore Point. On the right the coastal marshes are given over to grazing. Most of this walk along the coast is on a timber walkway. This is to reduce the erosion of the soft light sand, nevertheless in places the boards are being covered by blown sand. The path comes very close to the sandy beach where the circle of ancient posts was discovered. As you approach The Firs, a house to the right of a clump of trees, the path veers slightly right down through the sand dunes.

3. Come to a boardwalk at right angles which leads to the beach on the left, and on the right to the Visitors' Centre of the Nature Reserve. Keep straight on through conifers. Near the end of the wood see, amid the trees, a bird hide on the right. Just beyond the wood turn sharp right up a boardwalk with several steps to the entrance to a bird observatory, and then turn left along the top of a bank. Below on the right is a long lake, called Broad Water.

4. On reaching the end of the lake on the right, pause at a seat to enjoy the magnificent panoramic view of the Norfolk coastline. The path bends round to the right away from the coast, following a creek. The salt marsh on the left is called Ragged Marsh. Later squeeze beside a

Gore Point

gate. At this point a grass path straight ahead towards the distant trees leads to the coast road.

5. Continuing the walk, turn left along the top of the bank forming the sea wall. Go beside another gate and note the well designed notice board illustrating how people on the sands can become cut off by the rising tide. Just after the gate the path on the sea wall continues, but turn left, cross a channel by a brick arch bridge and drop down on to a surfaced road at marsh level. Occasionally the road can become flooded at high spring tides. In that case keep on the path at the top of the sea wall.

Walk along the road. As you pass, notice the attractive storage building beside a quay built of a mixture of materials, brick, flint, and brown carstone. Pass a timber bridge over a dyke on the left where the Norfolk Coast Path continues but keep straight on along the road. At the junction with Ship Lane go straight on unless you want to go to the Lifeboat Inn or the centre of Thornham.

6. Reaching the A149, the main coast road, turn left to pass a fine house behind old iron railings and then turn right along Ringstead Road, passing several chalk-faced buildings. Gradually climb for about ½ mile and then turn right along a road signed to Ringstead. Look through gaps in the hedge on the right to see across to the coastline. In about ½ mile come to a junction on the right by an old OS trig point. Keep straight on. In the distance half right is the tower of Holme church.

7. In about 200 yards where the road bends half left, keep straight on along a Peddars Way Circular Walk (as waymarked) on a broad grassy lane between hedges. This pleasant lane called 'Green Bank' on the map is at the edge of a plateau, flat on the left but sloping down to the coastal plain on the right. A track leads off to the right but keep straight on.

8. When you come to a road, turn left. In about 100 yards, at the edge of Ringstead, turn right at a Peddars Way signpost along a headland path with a hedge on the left. At the corner of a field turn right towards the coast, as signed. After a bit there is a hedge on the left and soon you are in a narrow lane with hedges on both sides. Follow the waymark and come out to a road.

9. Cross straight over and follow the road signed Holme Beach. Pass a road off to the right to Holme village but keep straight on and return to the start.

PLACES OF INTEREST NEARBY

On the route is the *Holme Dunes Nature Reserve & Visitors' Centre* of the Norfolk Wildlife Trust. Open daily 10 am to 5 pm. Permits to view the reserve can be obtained from the gift shop. Telephone: 01485 525240. Eight miles south is *Great Bircham Windmill*. The mill, five floors high together with gift shop and tea room, is open daily, except Monday and Tuesday, between April and October. Telephone: 01485 578393.

BRANCASTER

Wonderful views accompany this sea walk – don't forget your binoculars! Starting from the edge of the beach, the walk follows the edge of the marshes and creeks to the staithe before turning inland past Burnham Deepdale church. After rising up a shallow valley, and passing pleasant beech woods, the walk crosses Barrow Common to return along a grassy lane to the Roman fort of Branodunum.

This part of the north Norfolk coastline comprises sand and shingle banks facing the sea, behind which a flat expanse of salt marsh is broken up by tidal creeks and inlets. It is ideal for walking and for birdwatching. A broad inlet extends to the staithe at Brancaster and an arm of the creek running parallel to the shore cuts off the shingle promontory, Scolt Head, from the mainland to form an island, which is a National Nature Reserve managed by English Nature. In the middle of the village is the site of the Roman fort of Branodunum.

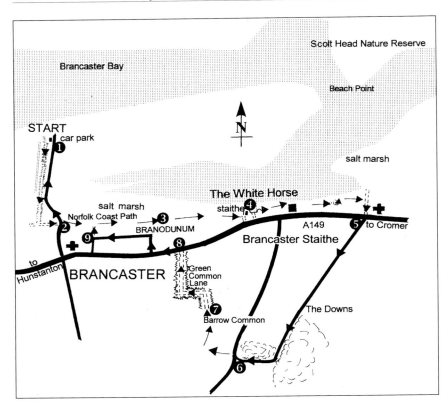

The White Horse at Brancaster Staithe is on the A149 main road. Look out for the inn sign that depicts the White Horse facing west. A cheerful welcome awaits you in the light and airy lounge and you can enjoy the view across the sea from the large windows in the restaurant area. Locally caught fish is a speciality here. Why not try their freshly cooked mussels? Telephone: 01485 210262.

- **HOW TO GET THERE:** Brancaster is half way between Hunstanton and Wells-next-the-Sea on the A149 coast road. At Brancaster church take the turning to Brancaster Beach.
- **PARKING:** There is a good car park at Brancaster Beach. As an alternative, there is a lay-by next to an AA box on the A149 coast road between Brancaster and Brancaster Staithe. If using the lay-by, you would join the circular walk at the staithe and reduce the length of the walk to about 6 miles.

- **LENGTH OF THE WALK:** 7 miles. Maps: OS Landranger sheet 132 North West Norfolk; OS Explorer 23 Norfolk Coast West (GR 771450).

THE WALK

1. From the Brancaster beach car park, walk out to and cross the road and climb the bank forming the sea wall (behind the toilet block) and turn left. Walk along the top of the bank parallel to the road. On the right is a drainage channel and behind it, flat arable land, while there is salt marsh on the left. Where the beach access road bends half left keep straight on along the sea wall, but soon the path drops down to the right off the wall and continues beside it. Go through a steel barrier and out to a lane and turn left.

2. At the road turn left for about 20 yards and at a National Trust sign turn right along a grass path which is part of the Norfolk Coast Path. Keep along the path at the edge of the marshes. Ignore a footpath leading off to the right. Pass an attractive looking house with a circular look-out tower, surmounted by a galleon weather vane. The marshes to the left are a haunt for a variety of sea birds.

3. Notice a stile on the right that leads into the site of Branodunum, a Roman camp. There is an information board here which will give you the background story. Keep straight on at the edge of the marsh, which here is lush grass and reeds and is used for grazing. After passing a fine looking brick and stone barn, now converted to a dwelling, go through a kissing gate and pass the end of a creek on the left. Beyond the creek come to a lane and turn left and pass the end of a row of brick cottages with decorative dormer windows. At the corner of the buildings on the right and beside the creek on the left, swing right to Brancaster Staithe.

4. Turn left towards the slipway for a few yards and turn right at the Norfolk Coast Path sign. Pass the end of another creek, with several moored boats, and swing left and right passing a stack of lobster pots and nearby some fishermen's huts. Continue along the coast path at the edge of the salt marsh for about ¾ mile. The path then makes a sharp bend to the left to skirt a slight hill forming a small promontory. Continue at the edge of the marsh. Very soon come to a creek and meet, at right angles, a hard track that runs out across the salt marsh. Turn right, away from the beach, along the cart track.

Some of the attractive houses at Brancaster staithe

5. Come out to the A149 road, close by a church. Cross the main road and take the minor road which is almost opposite. Pass Dale End, an estate road, on the right. The road climbs up a shallow hill. After about ½ mile you come to a wood on the left and, a little further, a stand of beeches on the right. Bend right along the road at the corner of the beech wood and follow it beside the wood on the right.

6. On reaching a road junction where there is a grass triangle, turn right for about 30 yards and then take the footpath on the left signed to Branodunum. This is a narrow grassy footpath across Barrow Common. Before long, having swung round to the right, the path lies at the edge of the common beside an arable field on the left. At the top of the hill there are fine views of the Norfolk coastline.

7. Leave Barrow Common through a gate and follow Green Common Lane, a wide drift way between hedges. The lane bends left and later bends right, and descends to the A149 just opposite the site of the Roman fort.

8. Turn left along the road for about 350 yards and turn right along Stockings Lane. Follow the lane and soon turn left into Cross Lane. Pass a road called Branodunum on the left and keep straight on.

9. In less than ½ mile at a T-junction turn right along Marsh Drove which leads back to the Coastal Path. Turn left and retrace your steps until you meet the road to the beach. Turn right and walk back to the beach car park and the start.

PLACES OF INTEREST NEARBY

A little to the west of Brancaster is *Titchwell Marsh*, a major RSPB bird reserve. The area attracts a great variety of birds at all seasons of the year. There are hides overlooking the sea creeks and marshes. An information centre, with a shop and picnic area is at the reserve. Telephone: 01485 210779.

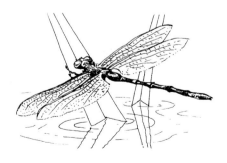

BURNHAM OVERY AND THE RIVER BURN

Lonely salt marshes and tidal creeks are the waterside attractions on this not-to-be-missed walk, which follows Overy Creek towards the sea and then a cart track inland across the pasture of the now drained coastal marsh. The walk continues on a cross-field path to the edge of Burnham Overy Town. Looping back to the head of the tidal creek, there is a short diversion to see, in a pretty setting, Burnham Overy Mill, an attractive building now tastefully converted into dwellings. Continuing across the marshes to the edge of Burnham Norton the walk returns via the sea wall back to the staithe.

The Staithe at Burnham Overy

This wide area of salt marsh, tidal creeks and coastal grazing is within a national Nature Reserve. In winter the area attracts flocks of Brent and pink footed geese, and redshank, snipe and lapwing live here. In the Middle Ages ships would sail 2 miles up the River Burn to Burnham

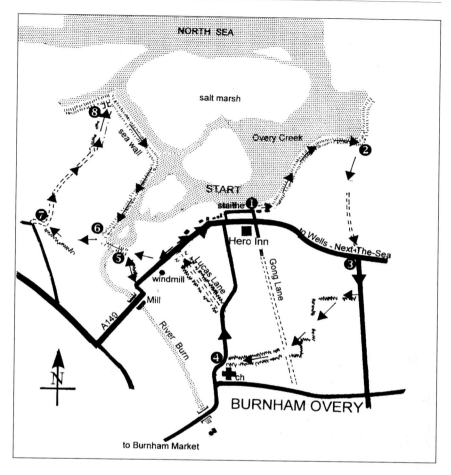

Overy Town. Over the years, however, the river has silted up to the extent that it is now a small stream and boats, small ones at that, can reach only as far as Burnham Overy Staithe. Five settlements, each including Burnham in its name, lie in the valley of the River Burn, the largest being Burnham Market, a pleasant village with a wide main street with a stream running nearby. Burnham Overy Town is now a tiny place on the bank of the river. There are the remains of a friary nearby and, further along the river, rather unusually, a windmill and a watermill (now converted) sharing the same site. Further upstream is Burnham Thorpe, the birthplace of Lord Nelson, the famous admiral.

Fronting the main A149 road in Burnham Overy Staithe is the Hero

Inn, serving home cooked meals in a pleasant and friendly atmosphere. Vegetarian options are included in the menu and children's tastes are also provided for. Telephone: 01328 738334.

- **HOW TO GET THERE:** Burnham Overy is on the A149, Hunstanton to Cromer, coast road about 5 miles west of Wells-next-the-Sea. Opposite the Hero public house, turn along East Harbour Way.
- **PARKING:** There is a parking area between the road and the creek, partly reserved for boats. There is also parking on the foreshore, but have regard to possible high tides. At peak holiday times it may become crowded here. In lieu of a fixed parking charge, drivers are asked to put a donation in a collecting pillar situated close to the access to the foreshore.
- **LENGTH OF THE WALK:** 6 miles. Maps: OS Landranger sheet 132 North West Norfolk; OS Explorer 24 Norfolk Coast Central (GR 844443).

THE WALK

1. From the corner where East Harbour Way meets the creekside highway, go eastward, along a grass path beside a brick house on the right. Note as you pass the converted granary and immediately after, the large house with Flemish gables. Turn left along the gravel path along the top of a grassy bank forming protection against flooding of the coastal marshes. I will call this the sea wall. Keep along the sea wall, beside Overy Creek for over ½ mile.

2. Where the path turns sharp left, turn right, dropping down off the sea wall. Negotiate a stile beside a gate and follow a grass track inland. Pass through a steel gate and later cross a two-step stile beside another gate, to continue along a cart track between hedges.

3. Duck through a steel gate and then cross the A149. Continue along the minor road and on reaching, in about 300 yards, the second hedge on the right, turn right along the headland with the hedge on the left. In about 150 yards, at a waymark, turn left over a bank and walk across the corner of the field towards a post on another bank.

Having crossed the second bank continue in the same direction on a cross-field path. Pass a waymark at an internal field corner and keep straight on. At the far corner of the large field come out to Gong Lane, a stony track. Go straight on along a grass path between hedges, which leads to a road at the edge of Burnham Overy Town.

4. Turn right and in about ¼ mile, where the road swings half right go straight on along a cart track, Lucas Lane. At the main road, cross straight over and turn left along a grass headland path beside the road. Before long turn half right across the field to a stile at the edge of the creek and climb the sea wall.

5. If you wish to make a short diversion to Burnham Overy Mill, turn left here and descend the bank, cross a stile and follow a hedge on the left. A stile takes you out to the A149 again. Turn right for a few yards and follow the road round to the left to see the watermill and the River Burn. Retrace your steps back to the sea wall.

Turn left along the wall, with the creek and salt marsh on the right. Soon pass the sluice gates where the River Burn discharges to the creek.

6. Where the sea wall turns sharp right, drop down and go straight on towards Burnham Norton, now along a bank between reed-edged ditches. At the end of the bank swing right along the edge of the marsh.

7. Cross a stile and turn right along a lane signed to the Coast Path. Go through gates beside a cattle crush and continue along a path between hedges. The track appears to end but turn right over a stile and continue, with a ditch on the left and a fence on the right.

8. Cross a wooden footbridge, climb the sea wall and turn right. In just over ½ mile you will be back at the head of the creek where you were earlier. Now you must return along the route you used previously to the end of Lucas Lane. Then keep along the grass path beside the main road on the right. This will bring you to a footway through the village, passing several cobble-faced cottages. Take the first turning to the left. Note as you pass an old wall with massive buttresses on the left, presumably the remains of the old maltings. In a short distance you will be back at the start.

PLACES OF INTEREST NEARBY

Three miles towards Wells is *Holkham Hall*, an 18th century mansion in a deer park. It was the home of the agricultural reformer Thomas Coke, 2nd Earl of Leicester. Open 1 pm to 5 pm Sundays to Thursdays from May to September, there are also a restaurant, gift shop and a bygones museum. Telephone: 01328 710227.

BLAKENEY

Our waterside walk begins in Blakeney itself, formerly a busy commercial wool port, but now a thriving sailing centre with many old timbered buildings and, just off the main street, the remains of a 14th century Guildhall. From Blakeney Harbour, we follow the sea wall eastward behind the Cley Channel, until we reach the shingle beach. The route then turns inland towards the village of Cley – now some ½ mile from the sea and passes Cley Windmill before heading back to Blakeney. This is a memorable walk – so don't forget your camera!

This stretch of the north Norfolk coastline between Hunstanton and Sheringham has quite rightly been designated an Area of Outstanding Natural Beauty. It is one of the most unspoilt parts of East Anglia and offers a wonderful landscape to all who enjoy the magic of open space, the calling of sea birds, the rustling of marshland grasses and reeds, and broad open skies.

Blakeney Point is a shingle spit which reaches out westwards along the coast. It has been a nature reserve for many years and there are

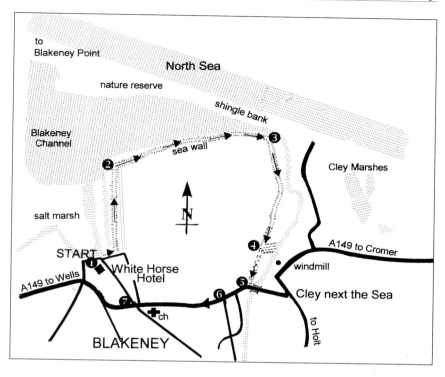

nesting colonies of birds to see at all times of the year. An excursion by boat to view the huge numbers of grey and common seals off-shore is a popular trip.

Being so close to the sea means that there are plenty of pubs and restaurants in Blakeney that offer a good range of fresh fish dishes. A short distance from the quay, up the HIgh Street, is the White Horse Hotel, and fish features prominently on its excellent menu. Telephone: 01263 740574.

- **HOW TO GET THERE:** Follow the A149 coast road between Wells and Sheringham, and take the turning to Blakeney Harbour.
- **PARKING:** There is a good car park almost on the beach at the eastern side of the harbour. An alternative car park is about 350 yards from the quay, along High Street.
- **LENGTH OF THE WALK:** 4 miles. Maps: OS Landranger sheet 133 North East Norfolk; OS Explorer 24 Norfolk Coast Central (GR 028442).

THE WALK

1. Walk to the eastern end of the quay and climb the shallow bank behind the sandy car park. At the top, you will find a gravel footpath along the flood protection bank. Go towards the sea. At first there is the car park area on the left and later, a dinghy park. About 50 yards away beyond the boats is a narrow channel that leads from the harbour to the open sea. On the right, below the bank, is a narrow drainage ditch.

2. You come to a place where the flood protection bank, or sea wall bends to the right. A few yards further walk past a stile on the right where a footpath leads back across the marshes to Blakeney. If you pause and look back here you will see the wide stretch of the Blakeney Channel which leads westward parallel to the coast for 3 miles to reach the open sea. Between the channel and the sea is Blakeney Point. Proceed ahead along the sea wall. The creek on the left becomes increasingly narrower. Over to the right, on a tree-lined hill, the tower of Blakeney church is clearly visible. It is easy to understand why the tower has long been a navigation aid for mariners.

3. The sea wall makes a sharp bend to the right. The creek on the left prevents you reaching the shingle spit of Blakeney Point and the River Glaven bars the way further east. You will now be walking with the River Glaven meandering through the salt marsh on the left. Ahead of you is Cley Windmill.

4. At the end of the bank on which you are walking, cross a gravel track at right angles and climb a rather higher bank. For a closer view of the windmill, turn left for a few yards, to a fence surrounding some sluice gates on the river. Then retrace your steps.

5. Continue along the bank and eventually you cross a stile beside a wooden gate to reach a road (the A149). If you want to explore the village of Cley and its windmill, then turn left here along the road for about 300 yards.

Continuing the walk, turn right along the footway beside the road. In about 200 yards pass a road on the left to Wiveton. Keep straight on along the road for another 200 yards, walking with care because there is no footway.

Cley windmill

6. When you reach another road junction, almost at the top of a hill, continue along the road, now using a footway on the north side of the road. St Nicholas' church is along here on the left. Notice that as well as the main church tower which you saw from the coast path, it has an unusual thin tower at the end of the chancel. A notice tells you that the tower is open on Fridays between 2 and 4 pm.

7. Not far beyond the church, you come to a five-way junction. Turn right along High Street, which is the second road on the right. This is a pleasant narrow village street with many attractive buildings. First, notice on the left a row of cobble-faced cottages. Further down the street are buildings alive with clematis and honeysuckle in summer. Pass the White Horse Hotel on the left as you approach the harbour. Just past the hotel, you can make a short diversion to the right, along a narrow passage to see the vaulted chamber of the ancient Blakeney Guildhall, before returning to the start.

PLACES OF INTEREST NEARBY
Boat trips to see the seals are run, dependent on tides, by several operators from Morston Quay just a mile west of Blakeney. Booking is advised. Telephone: 01263 740038; 740791; or 740753. There are demonstrations of decorative glass blowing and other crafts at *Langham Glass*. Take the B1156 south from Blakeney, and look out for signs. Open daily, April to October; in winter, Mondays to Fridays. Telephone: 01328 830511.

SHERINGHAM AND WEST RUNTON

᠁

Expect great views on this coastal outing, as after starting along Sheringham's promenade, this lovely cliff-top walk follows the Norfolk Coast Path towards West Runton. From the village, the return is up through National Trust woodland to Beeston Regis Heath and then descending along a shady path through Sheringham Woods back to the town centre.

The foreshore at West Runton

Cliffs of compacted sand flank the town of Sheringham – in this area there is a constant battle against coastal erosion. Sheringham itself is protected by sea walls incorporating fine promenades. To the south of the town, the land rises to a range of wooded hills which form an attractive backdrop to the local coastal settlements. Traditionally Sheringham, with its neighbouring town of Cromer, is noted for the crab fishing industry. During the season, from March to October, crab boats set out from the beach in the early hours of the morning to collect the crabs trapped in wicker pots in pools on a submerged platform of chalk rock a little offshore.

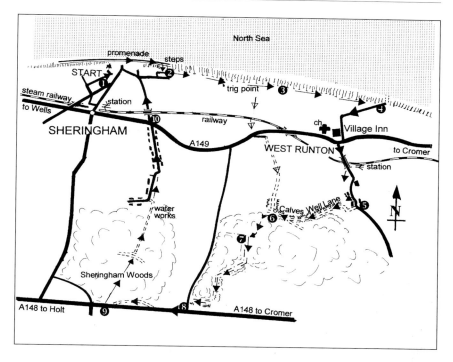

Approached through a broad garden and conveniently situated along the walk, is the Village Inn at West Runton. Built in the 1920s for a golf club, there are two bars and a restaurant. Tasty food, in generous portions, is served in a warm and friendly environment. Telephone: 01263 838000. Just back from Sheringham Promenade, on Lifeboat Plain, is Ye Olde Tea Room. Uniformed waitresses serving delicious cream teas and other light meals, remind one of an earlier age when small intimate cafés like this were quite common. Telephone: 01263 821532.

- **HOW TO GET THERE:** Sheringham lies on the A149 coast road between Cromer and Wells-next-the-Sea. Turn north at a roundabout on the A149 close to the town centre.
- **PARKING:** There are several car parks in the town but the one recommended is just west of the main street. To get there turn left opposite the British Rail station and then turn right opposite the old station, now the terminus of the private North Norfolk Railway. Follow the 'P' signs through several junctions.

- **LENGTH OF THE WALK:** 6½ miles or 5 miles. Maps: OS Landranger sheet 133 North East Norfolk; OS Explorer 25 Norfolk Coast East (GR 157433).

THE WALK

1. From the car park go back to the road and turn right. Turn left at the T-junction and after passing the end of a slipway, bear right to the concrete promenade. Turn right on a bridge over the slipway and continue along the lower promenade. Before long, pass the top of another slipway and keep along East Promenade. Climb steps up to the right, just by a tall square building built into the cliff. At the top of the steps continue up a concrete ramp to a road.

2. Go left, at the sign, towards Beeston Hill. The road ends and you climb a gravel track beside a putting green. After the first rise you may care to pause at a seat and look back at the coastal view over Sheringham. The grassy cliff-top path continues up to the top of a hill where there is an old OS trig point, now disused, and some more seats. Descend the hill, still on the cliff path and cross a field to the boundary of a caravan site. Here the right of way turns inland but you can continue along the cliff top on a permissive path.

The soft sandy cliffs are constantly eroding and there may well come a time when the permissive path ahead is lost to the sea. If the path cannot be used, or if you wish for a shorter walk, turn right and walk inland. Cross the railway and, following the Norfolk Coast Path, rejoin the route at a four-way sign (see paragraph 6).

3. The full walk continues straight on, along the narrow cliff-top path, at first between a pond on the right and steep cliff on the left, and then beside the caravan park. Before long reach the Laburnum Caravan Park and here keep beside a fence on the left at the top of the cliff. Beyond the caravans, still keep in the same direction and walk across an open space, descending to a cliff-top car park, where a ramp leads down to the beach. This is West Runton.

4. Turn right along the road, Water Lane, and walk into the village, later passing the Village Inn on the right. At the T-junction, cross the main road, turn right and immediately turn left along Station Road. Cross the railway bridge by West Runton Station and at the far end of the bridge approach; take the footpath, roughly parallel to the road,

Sheringham from Barrow Hill

across West Runton Common. Pass the Links Hotel away to the left. The path over the common swings left and brings you back to the road at the entrance to the West Runton Shire Horse Centre. Follow the road, soon to pass a fine terrace of cobble-faced cottages, on the right.

5. Immediately after the buildings turn right along Calves Well Lane, signed to Beeston Regis. After about 100 yards turn sharp right, along the gravel track. The lane gradually bends left and later runs beside a wood, mainly of oak and sweet chestnut trees, on the left. In the distance on the right you can see Beeston Hill, where you were earlier. Ignore several minor paths entering the wood on the left but notice (about ¼ mile from the start of this lane) a track coming in obliquely from the left. There is a two-arm signpost opposite it. Continue along the lane for a further 200 yards to a four-way junction where the main track bends right.

6. At this point turn left into the wood on a narrow bridleway, signed to Beeston Heath. As you walk through the wood, do not be diverted by National Trust footpath waymarks to left and right. Very soon after the four-way junction the narrow bridleway bends right, and within view of a dwelling on the right, bears left through a shallow valley.

After climbing steadily through the wood for about 350 yards along a narrow path, which tends to bend to the right at the end, you come to a place where several tracks meet. Go straight ahead for a few yards. Here you need to find the corner of a wire netting fence, relatively new and in good condition, round a part of the wood. Here you turn left.

7. Walk the narrow path beside the fence on your right, going almost due south. In 200 yards reach another corner of the fence. Turn half-right and continue beside the fence. On the left is a belt of trees beyond which is an open field. Eventually you reach a path junction beside the third fence corner. Turn right and still follow the fence. The path leads out to a road. Turn left and in 100 yards reach the A148 main road at a T-junction.

8. Turn right along the verge. To avoid the main road bear right along a minor road to the Household Waste site. Keep on the road, which soon returns you to the A148, and continue for a further 100 yards.

9. Immediately opposite a road sign reading 'P. Pretty Corner Tea Gardens' turn right, climb a slight bank and follow a lovely path through Sheringham Woods, going downhill between two shallow banks. On reaching a track at right angles, go left and then right to continue along a broader path which leads past an information board and then on, between water works buildings to continue as a surfaced access road. Where the access road joins a housing estate road, keep straight on along a parallel path to come out to the road in about ¼ mile. Keep straight on along Common Lane to the A149 main road.

10. Cross straight over and walk along Beeston Lane, going under the railway. After passing several terraces of pebble-faced cottages (characteristic of this area), come to the junction with Cliff Road, where you bear left for a short distance to reach the main shopping street. Turn left to the Clock Tower and turn right. Turn right opposite the Little Theatre Bar along a lane to return to the car park.

PLACES OF INTEREST NEARBY

The walk passes the *Shire Horse Centre*, at West Runton, open March to October. You can meet the animals and see the horses working. There are also cart rides. Telephone: 0263 837339. South of West Runton lies 17th century *Felbrigg Hall*, (National Trust), a large mansion set in picturesque surroundings. Telephone: 01263 837444.

HORSEY MERE AND THE NORTH SEA

Here the Broads come within a mile or so of the sea, and this lovely walk gives you the best of both worlds. Look out for seals on the beach as you follow the coastal path, then turn inland towards beautiful reed-fringed Horsey Mere and its picturesque old mill. Waterside and field paths, and a visit to Horsey's ancient little church, bring you back to Horsey Gap.

Brograve Drainage Mill and Waxham New Cut

The tiny, isolated village of Horsey is just a mile from the North Sea and as you walk you will be aware of how vulnerable this flat, low-lying land is to inundation by the sea – the high sand dunes covered with marram grass are a vital part of the sea defences. Yet nearby, situated as it is at the north-eastern edge of the Norfolk Broads, cruisers and other small craft sail across Horsey Mere to the staithe alongside

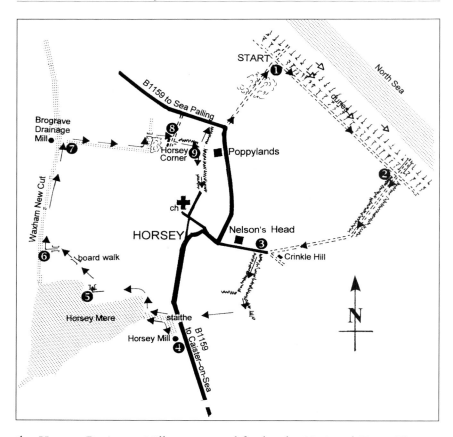

the Horsey Drainage Mill, now cared for by the National Trust. Horsey Mere is a wonderful spot, full of life and interest from the waterborne craft. The mill is open daily, April to September (telephone 01263 733471 to check times).

In a converted barn, Poppylands Tea Rooms is just off the route of the walk. Light refreshments are served with home-made cakes a speciality. The flint walls are decked with attractive paintings for sale and craft goods are sold upstairs. If you would like different fare, Austrian specialities such as Wiener schnitzel and Znaimer Gullet with noodles (beef cooked in paprika) figure on the menu at the Nelson's Head, at Horsey. No doubt in recognition of the opportunities for bird watching in this area, the Nelson's Head also offers a Twitchers' Lunch (ham, cheddar, pate or smoked mackerel served with salad, pickles and roll). Telephone: 01493 393378.

- **HOW TO GET THERE:** Horsey is between Winterton-on-Sea and Sea Palling on the north-east Norfolk coast. Coming from the south along the B1159, after bends to the right through the village, you make a sharp left turn by a telephone kiosk. In about ½ mile, where the road makes a second sharp left turn, go straight on along an unsigned gravel track to the car park.
- **PARKING:** National Trust car park (free at present) at the edge of the sand dunes at Horsey Gap. Alternatively there is a surfaced National Trust (pay and display) car park at Horsey Mill. For those who park here, follow the walk description starting at paragraph 4.
- **LENGTH OF THE WALK:** 5 miles. Maps: OS Landranger sheet 134 Norwich and The Broads; OS Outdoor Leisure 40 The Broads (GR 464241).

THE WALK

1. The public footpath leaves at the right hand (south-east) side of the car park. However, if you would like to start with a look at the sea, first take the sandy track straight ahead and walk through the dunes to the beach. It is possible to walk along the shore, but probably the best route is along the public footpath, diverting from time to time across the dunes to see the sea, as the public are asked to protect the sea defences by using the pathways provided. You may be lucky enough to see seals on the beach, but please leave them undisturbed.

2. In a little over ½ mile, you will come to a place where a narrow track runs through the dunes to the beach. This is another opportunity of reaching the shore. Massive concrete retaining walls support the sand dunes on both sides of the track and great baulks of timber look ready to close off the gap in times of storm. Note the plaque commemorating the completion of the sea defence works in 1988. Leave the coast here, following the grassy path between hedges which leads inland from the track through the dunes. Pass through a gap beside a steel gate and then continue along a stony track between reed-edged ditches. On reaching Crinkle Hill, an isolated pair of houses on the left, join a surfaced road.

3. In less than 100 yards turn left along a grass path between hedges. This National Trust permissive path leads directly to Horsey Mill, and is open during the summer. Go into a meadow at the end of the lane and continue beside a ditch on the left. Clamber over a stile at the field corner and immediately turn right beside a ditch, and walk towards the mill. At the road, cross straight over to reach the staithe.

If you are walking in winter when the path is unavailable, keep straight on along the road, pass the Nelson's Head and soon join the B1159. You can walk along the road to the mill.

4. On the left is the picturesque Horsey Drainage Mill – the low pumping station building almost adjacent is the modern equivalent. A short diversion round the end of the staithe, passing the mill and keeping beside the waterway on the right, brings you to a grassy sward with a delightful view of Horsey Mere.

Retrace your steps to the mill. To continue the walk, take the footpath beside the water on your left to the end of the staithe. Turn right and the path continues, separated from the mere by an extensive reed bed. Later you can catch glimpses, over the reeds, of the extent of the mere.

5. Eventually you make a sharp turn to the right, drop down some steps, cross a boardwalk and go over a stile in to a meadow. Make for a white spot on a stick at the far side of the field. Here you cross another stile, followed by a boardwalk. Continue along a narrow grass path through a reed bed. Shortly, bear left by another white spot and cross a further boardwalk.

6. Soon after the path turns to the right, you will reach the side of a wide ditch, known as Waxham New Cut. The map shows this waterway as navigable but you will probably find it very peaceful. Keep alongside the waterway for about ½ mile.

7. On the opposite bank of the Waxham New Cut you can see a derelict windmill, known as Brograve Drainage Mill. Turn right over a stile opposite the mill and continue along a headland path with a wide drainage ditch on the right. On the left are overhead electricity wires. The orange balls attached to the wires are a warning to birds thus indicating that you are crossing a flight path between the coast and inland open water. Cross a stile at the field boundary and still follow the drainage channel. Approaching the wood, swing left and then turn right over a stile. Cross a bridge and continue beside the wood on the right. Keep straight on to meet a road at Horsey Corner.

The beach at Horsey Gap

8. Turn right and almost immediately turn left along a cart track. The path continues with a hedge on the left. At the end of the field turn left at a T-junction of tracks.

9. At this point, a short diversion along the cart track to the right will take you to All Saints church, Horsey. Set in a pleasant quiet churchyard, it is a simple thatched church with a round flint tower surmounted by an octagonal section. Having seen the church, retrace your steps.

To complete the walk, go out to the road, Turn right for about 100 yards and then left along the unmade track that will bring you back to the car park.

PLACES OF INTEREST NEARBY

Follow the brown 'Duck' signs from Hickling to find the Norfolk Wildlife Trust's *Hickling Broad Visitor Centre, Nature Trail and Nature Reserve.* From Easter 2000 it will open daily 10 am to 5 pm except Tuesdays. Telephone 01692 670779.

THE NORTH WALSHAM AND DILHAM CANAL AT EAST RUSTON

A peaceful canal which has been cleared to encourage wildlife is the main attraction on this quiet walk through an unspoilt part of Norfolk, where the scenery is typical of the edges of Broadland beyond the reach of boat traffic. You return along part of the Weavers Way, a long distance path whose name recalls a time when this area's wealth depended on wool.

East Ruston canal

As far back as the 14th century, the nearby market town of North Walsham was a centre of the wool trade, and the size of the parish church is said to reflect the wealth that wool and weaving brought to the area. Much later, the North Walsham and Dilham Canal linked the town to the River Ant and the navigable river system, and thus to the world beyond. Over the years the canal fell into disuse and became

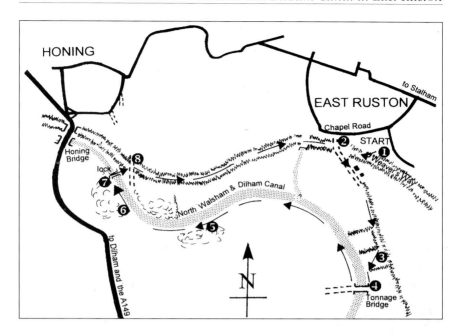

stagnant and overgrown, but recent conservation efforts have brought much of it back to life. The walk gives a fascinating contrast between 'before' and 'after' conservation. The route starts and finishes along part of the Weavers Way, a name that recalls the work of the past. This 56 mile long distance path joins Cromer and Great Yarmouth. The section of the path used here through East Ruston and neighbouring parishes makes use of a former railway track.

East Ruston is 3 miles from the A149 along minor roads. The Butcher's Arms is a comfortable and popular village pub with traditional décor. It has a separate restaurant in a bright room overlooking a vine-covered arbour. The menu offers a variety of roast dishes and an assortment of home-made pies. Beef stew and dumplings is also served. Telephone: 01629 650237.

- **HOW TO GET THERE:** East Ruston is a small village 5 miles south-east of North Walsham, on an unclassified road. At Smallburgh on the A149, south of North Walsham, take the road signed to Dilham. In about 2 miles, cross the canal on a narrow bridge. Take the first turning right at the common, and continue round two bends to the left. At the T-junction go right along East Ruston Road. In about

57

½ mile, after many bends, turn right and then in 220 yards turn right at the crossroads into Chapel Road. Go through the village and look out for a 'P Weavers Way' sign.

- **PARKING:** A small public car park beside the Weavers Way at the southern edge of East Ruston village.
- **LENGTH OF THE WALK:** 3½ miles. Maps: OS Landranger sheet 133 North East Norfolk; OS Outdoor Leisure 40 The Broads (GR 346272).

THE WALK

1. Starting from the Weavers Way car park at East Ruston, walk up to the Weavers Way path, which is along the former railway line. Turn right along the path for about 100 yards and pass through a gate on to a gravel drive which crosses the Weavers Way.

2. Turn sharp left along a track on a short length of permissive path. Soon you will pass a flint-faced cottage on the left, followed by a newer bungalow. Walk through a gate beside a steel farm gate, into a large field. With a hedge on the left, follow the cart track through a meadow, decked in season with clumps of irises. At the field boundary on the far side of the meadow, enter a short lane fenced on both sides, which leads into a field.

3. Walk diagonally across the meadow to cross a rickety stile beside a gate. Here you reach the North Walsham and Dilham Canal, which is a pleasant waterway fringed with mature alder trees and you will be following its course for the next part of the walk. Keep beside the canal on your right for 100 yards or so and, after a stile, reach Tonnage Bridge.

4. Turn right across the bridge and turn right again to continue along the opposite bank of the canal, now going upstream towards North Walsham. At the end of the first big field, go through a small wooded area. Cross a plank bridge over a small ditch. Here and for the next part of the walk you can see the results of the conservation work carried out along the canal. The alder trees have been thinned and coppiced and waterside shrubs removed to bring more light to the watercourse, and silt and detritus have been removed. The result is a canal flowing with bright clear water. You will cross several plank bridges over ditches as you follow the bank of the canal.

5. Pass, on the left, a small conifer wood. The absence of greenery on the trees facing the canal indicates that the trees closest to the water have been removed to let in more light. Soon after, there is a marshy wooded area on the left where the trees are mostly alders. The path leads through what can best be described as a squeezer gate, into a broad marshy meadow with isolated trees dotted around. Keeping beside the canal you will come to a wide ditch crossed by a gated timber bridge.

6. Continue beside the canal. After crossing another narrow ditch you enter a marshy alder wood through another squeezer gate. Here the canal is heavily shaded by vegetation and is badly silted. Clearly, at the time of writing, the conservation work has not reached this point.

7. When you come to disused Honing Lock, cross the water on a timber bridge over a weir at the upstream end of the lock, and leave the canal. A short distance after crossing another timber bridge, you meet a cart track. Turn left for a few yards and then turn right, to join the Weavers Way.

8. Continue along the former railway line for about ½ mile. The Weavers Way passes through a marshy wood and crosses a stream on a bridge with steel railings. Pass, on the right, a fishing lake and go through a gate. After passing a terrace of attractive flint-faced cottages on the left you will reach the gravel drive you used earlier. Keep straight on through a gate, back to the car park and the start.

PLACES OF INTEREST NEARBY

To the south-east, and just beyond Stalham, is *Sutton Windmill*, Britain's tallest windmill. For details telephone 01692 581195. Or why not visit the nearby small market town of *North Walsham*. There is a fine Tudor market cross in the town square, and an impressive church.

THE RIVER BURE AT BUXTON

The first part of this attractive walk is along a footpath following the Bure Valley Railway – look out for steam engines, or perhaps have a ride yourself! You then join the path along the banks of the delightfully clear River Bure on a circular route back to Buxton, enjoying woods and meadows and spotting some of the old mills that once dotted this landscape.

Buxton Mill

From its source near Melton Constable the River Bure flows through Aylsham, meandering past the villages of Buxton and Brampton and through a shallow valley to Wroxham and thence to the sea at Great Yarmouth. Plants in the river include starwort and watercress, indicating that the water is relatively free of pollution. You will probably spot an unusually large number of horses in the riverside meadows on this walk and it seems that the farms in this valley concentrate on breeding horses. The Bure Valley Railway is a 15-inch

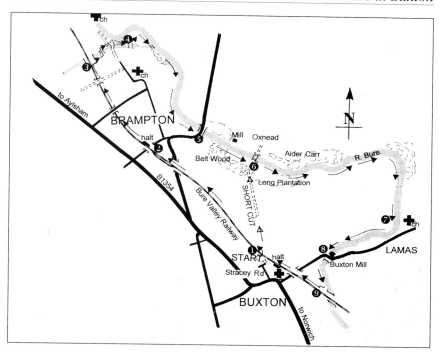

gauge railway built in 1990 on a 9 mile route of a former line between Aylsham and Wroxham, operated today mainly by steam locomotives. An interesting alternative, if your times allow, could be to ride the train between Buxton and Brampton Halt, thus reducing the walk by about 1 mile. (Telephone 01263 733858 for details.) An even shorter walk is available by taking a direct route to the river from the start.

The old weatherboarded Buxton Mill has been tastefully converted into the Mill Hotel. Walk out over the water along a timber walkway to enter the spacious bar and restaurant. As a reminder of the mill's industrial heritage, an old Lister oil engine stands proudly in the bar! Among the interesting items on the menu are oven roasted duckling with plum sauce, medallions of pork, avocado topped with prawns and Stilton, and venison steak. Telephone: 01603 278194.

- **HOW TO GET THERE:** Buxton is on the B1354 road between Aylsham and Coltishall. Pause at the parish church.
- **PARKING:** The Bure Valley Car Park, free at present, is adjacent to the Buxton Halt on the Bure Valley Railway and is approached

61

through a housing estate. Just west of Buxton church, turn north along Stracey Road. Soon turn right at a T-junction, and at the end of the road enter the car park.

- **LENGTH OF THE WALK:** 5½ miles, with a 3½ mile alternative. Maps: OS Landranger sheet 133 North East Norfolk; OS Pathfinder 862 Norfolk Broads (North) (GR 232228).

THE WALK

1. From the car park go through a small pedestrian gate and cross the railway line.

For the short walk, the route is straight ahead through a wooden barrier and across the field on a grassy path. After passing a concrete hardstanding, keep along a cart track, and later join a stony farm track. You join the main walk beside a cart bridge over the River Bure (see paragraph No 6 below).

For the full walk turn left beside the railway. Before long you pass a 3-mile post beside the line. Cross over a road on the old railway bridge, and still follow the railway track. Note the railway-passing loop.

2. Soon you will pass over another road and reach Brampton Halt. In about 450 yards go under a brick arch bridge. Continue, later under a three-arch bridge.

3. Just before the railway crosses a steel bridge over a small stream in a shallow valley, you turn right, to descend a flight of steps to a stile and the stream. Walk beside the stream on the left. Turn left and then right over a culvert to follow the stream on the right. At the field corner cross a timber bridge over a watercourse. After crossing a well-used track to the church, follow a very narrow path through a mixed plantation of trees. A stile at the end of the wood leads into a broad meadow.

4. Keep beside the stream on the right and later note, but do not cross, a cart bridge over it. In a short distance bear half left to a stile beside a wooden gate. Here you meet the River Bure just by a weir and sluice gates. Follow the riverbank, cross a bridge over a tributary and continue on a winding route through a wood, still beside the river on the left. Pass through three riverside fields, crossing stiles en route. Eventually you will climb between concrete cubes up to a road beside a narrow steel bridge.

The River Bure

5. Cross the road and drop down over a stile to another meadow. Now follow the river again and soon continue through a poplar plantation. A few yards to the left of the path look out for the walls of an old lock in a silted up channel beside the river. On reaching a meadow, you will be able to see a renovated mill building across the river. Leave the meadow at a stile and cross a stony farm track that leads to a bridge over the river.

6. Those taking the short walk will have come along the track to the right and if you wish, this path will take you directly back to the start. The walk continues through mixed woodland along the bank beside the River Bure on the left. At the end of the wood cross a stile and keep beside the river. The many poplar trees are an attractive feature of the river valley. Crossing several stiles on the way, continue along the riverside path, winding round a great loop towards Lamas and Buxton.

7. Eventually you will pass Lamas church, situated on the opposite side of the river, and shortly after, see a tall crinkle-crankle wall around a garden close to the church. Cross a stile into some uncultivated land and pass an ancient willow tree. Later cross another stile beside some dwellings on the right. Loop right, round a cottage on the riverbank. Look out for a pair of pulley wheels beside the front door. Then pass on the left the white weatherboarded restored mill building (now the Mill Hotel) and walk out to the road.

8. Go straight over the road and cross the stile. Continue beside the river on the left. After a slight bend, you will see ahead a steel girder bridge that carries the railway line. At the corner of the meadow cross a bridge over a wide ditch. Immediately swing right and again almost immediately turn left up steps to reach the Bure Valley Path beside the railway.

9. Divert a short distance to the bridge, to enjoy a good view of the river with Buxton Mill in the distance. Retracing your steps, follow the path beside the railway on the left, back to Buxton Halt and the car park.

PLACES OF INTEREST NEARBY

Just over a mile from Aylsham is magnificent *Blickling Hall* (National Trust). A large stately home set in an extensive park with lavish gardens, it is a major attraction in the area. The park is open daily and the house on afternoons April to October, but not Monday and Tuesday. Telephone for details: 01263 738030.

LUDHAM AND WOMACK WATER

This short walk follows the edge of Womack Water and then the bank of the River Thurne. The path continues beside drainage ditches as it skirts a National Nature Reserve where, among other things, rare dragonflies can be found. Binoculars would be very useful on this walk!

Womack Drainage Mill and the Horse Fen

Years ago, Womack Water was a small Broad to the south of the village of Ludham, connected by a short channel to the River Thurne. As has occurred throughout the Broads, progressive silting and the consequent spreading of reed beds and other vegetation, have reduced the area of open water in Womack Water. Now there is just a narrow channel between the boat yard by the staithe and the main waterway of the River Thurne. That will not lessen your enjoyment of this waterside walk, combined with the interest of Ludham Marshes nature reserve. Elsewhere much of this kind of habitat has been lost to plants and wildlife due to changing patterns of agriculture and animal husbandry.

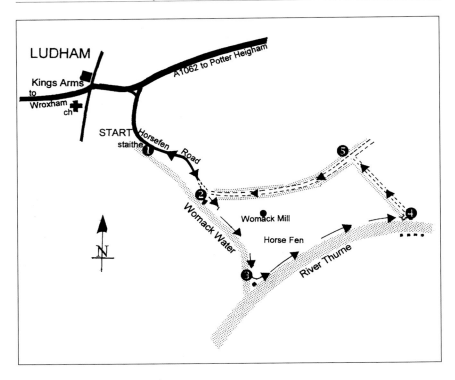

Standing at the crossroads in Ludham is the King's Arms, a traditional village pub serving food from its comprehensive menu. As well as a range of steaks, several vegetarian dishes, and a wide choice of pizzas on the regular menu, the blackboard of 'specials' offers many more interesting dishes, such as breast of chicken marinaded in citrus juice and wrapped in bacon and cheese. Telephone: 01692 678386.

- **HOW TO GET THERE:** Ludham is on the A1062 road between Horning and Potter Heigham, a mile west of Potter Heigham. From the crossroads in the centre of the village go about 250 yards towards Potter Heigham and turn right along narrow Horsefen Road.
- **PARKING:** On the right of Horsefen Road, immediately beyond a boat yard, is a staithe beside Womack Water. The car park is beside the staithe. There are public toilets here.

- **LENGTH OF THE WALK:** 2½ miles. Maps: OS Landranger sheet 134 Norwich and The Broads; OS Outdoor Leisure 40 The Broads (GR 391180).

THE WALK

1. From the staithe, where Broads cruisers moor, go out to the Horsefen Road and turn right. On the right, you pass partly thatched Womack House, and nearby two interesting barns, pebble-faced and thatched.

2. After passing the entrance to Swallowtail Boatyard on the right, you come to the end of the surfaced Horsefen Road, by Hunter's Yard. Follow the public footpath, which runs beside the fence of Hunter's Yard on the right. Before long you will find the path is following the bank of Womack Water, the watercourse on the right. The area of flat fields on the left, criss-crossed with drainage channels is Ludham Marshes, a National Nature Reserve. The dykes or ditches between the

In full sail on Womack Water

fields support a wide variety of wetland plants and animals, some of them rare – in particular the Norfolk Aeshna dragonfly. Your binoculars will enhance your enjoyment of this part of the walk. Prominent on the marsh is a disused drainage windmill.

3. As you get closer to the confluence with the River Thurne, the waterway bears left, away from the path. Soon after, the footpath bends left round a tree-fringed dwelling and meets the bank of the Thurne. Follow the riverbank for over ½ mile, with the Nature Reserve on your left. Eventually you will come to a row of chalets with their landing stages on the opposite bank of the river. In about 100 yards leave the riverbank, going left past the Horse Fen Pumping Station, the modern successor to the old drainage windmill.

4. Cross a steel bridge over a wide ditch and turn left along a cart track beside a dyke on the left. Later, go through a gate and very soon come out to a track at right angles. Turn left along a grassy cart-track between drainage dykes. In early summer these ditches are bright with flowers, particularly yellow flags and periwinkle.

5. After a while the lane swings round to the right, and you reach the end of Horsefen Road by Hunter's Yard. Walk up the road back to the start.

PLACES OF INTEREST NEARBY

North of Wroxham on the A1151 are *Hoveton Hall Gardens*, with lovely woodland and lakeside walks amongst rhododendrons and azaleas. There is a café for light meals. Open Easter to September, Wednesday, Friday and Sunday. Telephone: 01603 782798. *Wroxham* is a good place from which to explore the Broads by boat. Several operators have small boats for hire by the hour or by the day. Short cruises also run from Wroxham. Telephone: 01603 782207.

WALK 15

UPTON AND SOUTH WALSHAM BROAD

There is so much of interest to see on this walk from Upton by beautiful South Walsham Broad and back along the meandering rivers Bure and Thurne. Sailing craft, dinghies and motor cruisers ply up and down the river, but out of the holiday season this is an isolated area where duck and wildfowl abound. The walk passes a nature reserve and there is a view of ruined St Benet's Abbey across the river.

Upton Staithe

The River Bure is navigable from Coltishall to Great Yarmouth where it connects to the rivers Yare and Waveney. It forms much of the northern part of the Norfolk Broads network of waterways, and flows through wide areas of low-lying reclaimed marsh criss-crossed by ditches. The landscape is dotted with old windmills from the days when wind power was used to drain the land, though this is now done

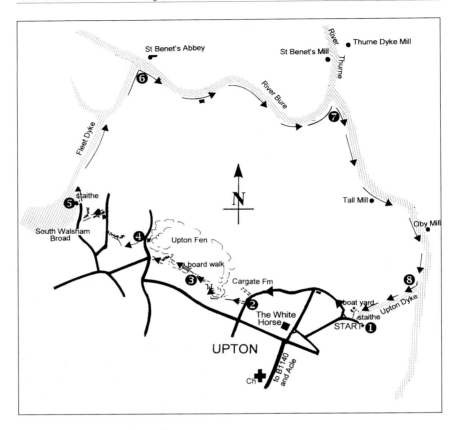

by electric pumps. St Benet's Abbey is a landmark for Broads sailors. It has been a ruin since the Dissolution in the 16th century, but the Bishop of Norwich is still nominally Abbot of the old foundation.

Not far from the staithe, the popular White Horse at Upton serves visitors from the Broads cruisers as well as the local people. Telephone: 01493 750696.

- **HOW TO GET THERE:** Upton is 1 mile north of Acle, on an unclassified road. Coming from the B1140 Acle to South Walsham road, keep straight on at the crossroads and turn right opposite the White Horse. Turn left and later swing right at a junction and go on to the end of the road.
- **PARKING:** A public car park lies at the head of Upton Dyke, near a boat yard. A grassed area with picnic tables adjoins the car park.

- **LENGTH OF THE WALK:** 7 miles. Maps: OS Landranger sheet 134 Norwich and The Broads; OS Outdoor Leisure 40 The Broads (GR 402129).

THE WALK

1. Leave the car park at Upton Dyke and walk back along the road. Turn right at the grass triangle, along Back Lane. In about ¼ mile, after passing a long brick building on the left, come to a road junction. Go straight on along Prince of Wales Road, passing several bungalows and later a house called the Old Prince of Wales. As you leave the village, the road is narrow and there are fields both sides.

2. After passing the entrance drive to Cargate Farm on the right, and immediately before Loke House, turn right along a cart track. The track becomes a narrow footpath and then a wider grassy path. Soon the path bends round and you are skirting the edge of an old wood. At the corner follow the path round to the right between the wood and a ditch. Cross a timber bridge, bear left and continue beside the wood.

3. Swing right along the path into the wood. This is soft marshy ground and, for a short distance, you use a narrow planked walkway. In spring the path here is edged with primroses. At the end of the wood continue along a grass path beside a hedge on the right. Turn right at the corner of the field, along a stony track between Holly Farm and Ivy Farm. On reaching a road, go right. In a short distance you pass the entrance to Upton Fen, a nature reserve of the Norfolk Wildlife Trust. Visitors are encouraged to follow a nature trail through the Alder Carr and young oak woodlands, while a display panel illustrates the wide variety of British dragonflies, but for now the walk continues ahead.

4. Opposite Marsh Lodge, a fine thatched brick building, turn left along a grass path and at the end of the field turn right, still on a narrow path between fields. At the field end, bear round to the left following a hedge on the right. When you reach a narrow road, turn right.

About 100 yards after passing thatched Town House Farm on the left, turn left over a stile without a footpiece and follow a grass path with a hedge on the left. At the corner continue straight on, now with a hedge on the right. Turn right along a road. Passing a car park, swing right along Fleet Lane to South Walsham Staithe, at South Walsham Broad.

5. After you have enjoyed the view of the Broad, keep along the road. It gradually deteriorates and soon becomes a grass footpath beside a landing stage fronting Fleet Dyke, the waterway giving access to the Broad. Pass the junction with another watercourse on the opposite side of Fleet Dyke. This was a former course of the River Bure.

6. About ½ mile from South Walsham Staithe, you reach the River Bure. Turn right, following the river bank. Across the river you will see, nestling against an old windmill, the ruined gatehouse of the Benedictine Abbey of St Benet. Some of the walls of the abbey itself are still visible east of the gatehouse. Pass a brick pumping station and you will see in the distance St Benet's Level Drainage Mill and a little to the left, by way of contrast, the smaller Thurne Dyke Mill. Further along the river bank you reach a second pumping station. Immediately beyond it is a track beside a wide drainage ditch that leads across the marshes, back to Upton.

7. Continue on the river bank for over ½ mile to the confluence with the River Thurne, flowing from Hickling Broad and passing Potter Heigham. This is a busy junction for boat traffic and there is always something to watch. On the right is the wide flat area of Upton Marshes. Follow the riverside path and pass, in about ½ mile, the Tall Mill, and later, the derelict Oby Mill on the opposite bank.

8. On reaching narrow Upton Dyke the path bends right beside the waterway. Continue alongside the dyke to return, via the boatyard and the staithe, to the car park.

PLACES OF INTEREST NEARBY

A visit to *Ranworth*, just a mile from South Walsham, is well worth while. A short walk along a nature trail leads to the Norfolk Naturalists Trust's *Broadland Conservation Centre*, where interesting displays are mounted and where visitors can easily observe the bird-life across the Broad. Telephone: 01603 270479. Also climb the *church tower* for a magnificent view of typical Broadland scenery. *Fairhaven Garden*, beside South Walsham Broad, is a woodland and water garden displaying a fine show of primroses and bluebells in the spring, with azaleas and rhododendrons later in the year. Open daily 10 am to 5 pm, telephone: 01603 270499.

WALK 16

FAKENHAM AND THE RIVER WENSUM

A delightful walk, combining the attractive little market town of Fakenham and a stroll along the banks of the River Wensum as it weaves through woods and past fields, enjoying the lush vegetation and mature trees, including some old coppiced willows.

A quiet spot to linger

The source of the River Wensum is a few miles south of Fakenham. After making a wide bend to the west and north, the river flows through Fakenham and then along a shallow valley across central Norfolk, to pass through Norwich. The Wensum joins the River Yare just south of the city. Fakenham is an attractive small market town. The compact market place and shopping area lies close to the river but the rest of the town has developed to the north of the river, leaving a narrow strip of potentially floodable land undeveloped.

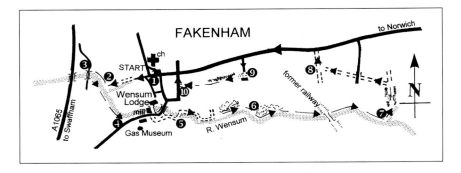

Fakenham Mill, built in 1750, lies on the route of the walk. In operation until the 1970s, it has now been attractively converted into dwellings. The adjacent granary building forms part of the Wensum Lodge Hotel, with restaurant and bar. Here you can relax in pleasant, bright surroundings. The somewhat original menu provides wide-ranging choice. For example, you can have medallions of monkfish; smoked haddock and asparagus spears; a speciality mixed grill is on offer, and many vegetarian dishes. Telephone: 01328 862100.

- **HOW TO GET THERE:** Fakenham, roughly in the middle of North Norfolk, lies on the A148 road between King's Lynn and Cromer. From Norwich use the A1067.
- **PARKING:** There are several car parks in Fakenham Town Centre. The most convenient is a North Norfolk District Council pay and display car park just south of the Market Place, in Bridge Street.
- **LENGTH OF THE WALK:** 3½ miles. Maps: OS Landranger sheet 132 North West Norfolk; OS Explorer 24 Norfolk Coast Central (GR 919296).

THE WALK

1. The walk starts at the Market Place in the centre of the town. Passing the War Memorial on your left, go in a westerly direction along the road. Where the main traffic turns right, keep straight on along Hall Staithe, a narrow road, passing on the left an attractive terrace of flint-faced cottages. Very soon notice on the right, the former fire station, now a garage, faced with decorative moulded brickwork. When the road ends continue on a gravel track, which soon becomes a surfaced footpath beside a small stream on the left.

2. Eventually the footpath bends right and follows the grassy bank of the River Wensum past many old coppiced willow trees.

3. On reaching a road turn left across the bridge. Immediately turn left and continue back along the opposite bank of the river. Here you are on a narrower, sandy path. About 250 yards from the bridge you should have a fine view of the parish church away to the left. A little further on, on the opposite bank, well-tended lawns sweep down to the river's edge.

4. The footpath ends at a road. Turn left along the footway. Soon you will see ahead the attractively converted building of the old Fakenham Mill. On the approach to the old mill look out for an old gasholder on the right. This is adjacent to the Fakenham Gas and Local History Museum, which you soon pass. The museum is usually open every Thursday during the summer months, 10.30 am to 3.30 pm, if you would like to look around.

Turn left beside the old mill, cross the river, and then loop round to the right, passing the former granary, now the Wensum Lodge Hotel. On returning to the road, turn right across the river-bridge, and make your way back along the road a short distance, passing a garage building. Just before the Gas Museum, make a U-turn left and go along the gravel yard behind the garage. This will bring you to a gravel track along the bank of the River Wensum.

5. Just by a recreation area with picnic tables on the right, follow the gravel track across the river on a concrete cart bridge. Now continue with the river on your right. Before long, leave the track which turns left towards some small sheds, and go straight on along a grass path, still keeping beside the river, which in summer is flanked with lush vegetation. There is a plantation of poplars on the left and a pleasant bench seat.

6. The river makes a bend to the right and the path rises slightly and passes between a pair of massive concrete fence posts. This is a clue that you are crossing a former railway line, and if you look at the riverbank you will see the remains of bridge abutments. The path descends slightly to a boardwalk beside the river and the river bends left. It is flanked by mature trees, making this a delightful walk. Keep along the riverbank, walking through an arch of a three-arch bridge over the river. This is another disused railway line which ran from East Dereham to Wells, but it did not connect with the old (Midland & Great Northern Joint Railway) line to Melton Constable you crossed earlier in the walk.

7. After keeping to the riverside for a further ¼ mile or so, the path swings left, following a small stream edged with reeds. Soon after, cross the stream on a substantial cart bridge with massive tall wooden railings on both sides. The path becomes progressively wider. Go through a gap beside a steel gate and turn left along a gravel road with houses on the right. Cross a housing estate road and keep straight on along Barbers Lane, still an unsurfaced track.

8. Barbers Lane ends at a T-junction of tracks. Turn right and walk out to the main road. Turn left along the footway. In a little over ¼ mile pass the entrance to a school and turn left along Barons Hall Lane.

9. At the end of the road go through a gateway and turn right in front of Barons Hall Farm. Leave the gravel farm drive and go straight on across rough ground to pass through a kissing gate into a pasture. Keep beside a fence on the right and at the field corner, another kissing gate leads into a wide gravel road. Keep straight on, passing a few industrial buildings on the left. Before long you are on a surfaced road.

10. Arriving at a T-junction, turn right and soon pass the side of Millers Walk Shopping Precinct on the left. Turn left at the mini roundabout. Continue along Norwich Road which will lead back to the Market Place.

PLACES OF INTEREST NEARBY

A major attraction in the area is the *Pensthorpe Waterfowl Park and Nature Reserve*. Situated a few miles from Fakenham on the A1067 towards Norwich, the park is centred around a series of lakes. There is an aviary and you can follow nature trails through the 200 acre site. Open daily March to December, 10 am to 5 pm, otherwise weekends only. Telephone 01328 851465.

A RIVERSIDE WALK THROUGH NORWICH

A fine walk through a fine city, the Norwich Riverside Walk gives you glimpses of the city's crowded past, passing the remains of medieval monastic buildings, ancient fortifications, and reminders of a proud industrial heritage. Take your time on this short walk to appreciate some of the delights that Norwich has to offer, guided by the River Wensum through its very heart.

Pulls Ferry

The River Wensum, a tributary of the River Yare, makes a broad loop through the centre of Norwich, fringing the cathedral close and passing through much of the historic core of the city. The Norwich Riverside Walk has been developed in the last 15 or so years and is almost complete. Attractive ceramic waymarks indicate the route. Please note that although developed by the Norwich City Council, some of the paths are gated and permissive, and notices indicate that gates are closed at dusk.

Beside Foundry Bridge is the Compleat Angler. This old coaching inn, known in 1845 as the Foundry Bridge Inn, is a pleasant establishment with tables outside overlooking the river. The menu offers, among other things, haddock and spinach Lyonaise; salmon tagliatelli and broccoli, pepper and Stilton crumble. Telephone: 01603 622425. Or you might like to try the restaurant at the Cathedral, where refreshments are served from 10 am to 4.30 pm.

- **HOW TO GET THERE:** The start of the walk is at Norwich Cathedral. Follow the pedestrian signs.
- **PARKING:** There are many town centre parking places in Norwich. Probably the most suitable is the large St Andrews multi-storey car park off St Andrews Street (follow the signs). A practical alternative is the city's Park and Ride service.
- **LENGTH OF THE WALK:** 2 miles. Maps: OS Landranger sheet 134 Norwich and The Broads; OS Outdoor Leisure 40 The Broads (GR 237089).

THE WALK

1. Enter the Cathedral precinct by the Erpingham Gate. Immediately in front of the west door of the cathedral, turn right along a footpath through a square with lawns and trees. Away on the left you will see the wall of the cloisters. Throughout the close are various reminders of the monastic foundation of the cathedral and in a short distance you will be walking beside the flint walls of the former cellarer's store rooms now part of Norwich School. At the corner of the buildings reach a road. On the right is the Ethelbert Gate, another of the four entrances to the cathedral close.

Turn left along the road and before long pass another grass square with fine Georgian buildings on the right. The dwellings on the left side of the square were originally part of the monastery buildings. Keep straight on beyond the square and later pass a long range of brick stables. A plaque on the right records that Sir Thomas Browne had a herb garden here. Norwich School playing field is passed on the left.

2. At the end of the road you are faced by a shallow arch in an old brick and flint building, through which you will see the river. This is Pulls Ferry and here a ferry used to ply across the River Wensum. The

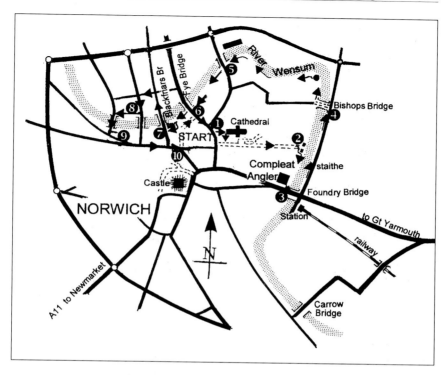

arch is interesting because it was built across a canal used to transport the stone to build the cathedral. The canal, filled in in 1782, followed the route of the road. Turn right through an iron gateway and very soon loop round to the riverbank. In about 300 yards, after passing some commemorative willow trees, climb steps and pass the Compleat Angler to reach Prince of Wales Road.

3. Turn left and cross Foundry Bridge, named after an iron foundry which stood on an adjacent site. Pause a moment to look half right to the palatial frontage of Thorpe Station, before turning left along Riverside Road.

The long landing stage on the left is the Norwich Yacht Station. This is, in practice, the western extremity of the Norfolk Broads network of waterways, and many visitors to Norwich moor their craft here. Towards the end of the Yacht Station take the first opportunity to drop down from the road to river level and walk beside the landing stage. As you approach the three-arch Bishop's Bridge, look out for a memorial to a number of Protestant martyrs who were burnt at the stake in Lollards Pit, later the site of the old gasworks. Climb back, beside the memorial, to Riverside Road and turn left.

4. Turn left over the pedestrianised Bishop's Bridge, which is the oldest river bridge in Norwich and immediately after, turn right along a short cul-de-sac. Do not enter the newish development but at the end of the road turn right and left and pick up, beside a hedge on the left, a gravel track. This passes through a gateway, back to the river bank, now on the right.

Very soon you will come to Cow Tower. This circular brick tower was part of the city's defences. Much of the City Wall remains to the north and west of the city centre but the river was deemed to be sufficient defence on the remaining sides, with the addition of this tower at the corner. The path continues along the river bank. Later cross a timber footbridge over a narrow ditch, which was linked to a swan pit. Swans reared here provided food for Cambridge Colleges. Go through a steel gate in a brick arch and after passing through a small riverside garden, walk through a pair of gates between massive brick piers. There is a high wall behind shrubs on the left.

On the opposite side of the river, its lower floor screened by willows, is St James' Yarn Mill. This magnificent building has an interesting history. There were many small companies of handloom weavers in the town in the early 19th century but they were suffering intense competition from steam-driven mills in the North. Samuel Bignold, the founder of the Norwich Union Insurance Co, built this steam-powered yarn mill, dividing the floor space so that the individual weavers could work using the communal power supply. Later the mill became a printing works.

5. Pass through a similar gateway to the last one, and after passing the entrance to the courts on the left reach Whitefriars Bridge. Cross the road and continue as before, on the riverside walk. Before long the path comes to a road at the edge of the river. The buildings on the left are mainly old warehouses, but include an old school. Keep along the road to a T-junction by the Rib of Beef public house. Fye Bridge is on the right.

6. Go almost straight over to continue, as before, with the river on the right. Pass a landing stage for river cruises. The riverside path runs into a car park. At the far end leave the riverside and take a paved path beside a brick building on the right. Turn left and walk a short distance between the remains of thick rubble walls which once formed part of the cloisters of Blackfriars Priory. Turn right and go out through an arch to a road and turn right. The brick building on the right was the Technical Institute in 1899 and is now the Art College.

7. Cross Blackfriars Bridge. A plaque records that the bridge was designed by Sir John Soane. Keep straight on, passing the Playhouse Theatre and continue to the crossroads. Turn left along Colegate and at the road junction, cross the pelican crossing and turn left.

8. Reach the river again at Dukes Palace Bridge. St Andrews multi-storey car park, on the far side of the bridge, is on the site of the Duke of Norfolk's Palace. Immediately before the bridge turn right down three steps and continue beside the river on your left. On the right is

St James's Yarn Mill

the site of the factory of Barnard, Bishop & Barnard, the inventors of wire netting.

St Miles Bridge is the next bridge. Turn left and cross the steel bridge. If you pause in mid span and look over the parapet on the upstream side you will see a casting attached to the parapet. This is a guide for a suction hose by which water could be extracted for fire fighting. Having crossed St Miles Bridge, turn left in about 50 yards and follow a new road under a wide arch in a building. Follow the road round to the right and at the end come to a preserved sign saying 'Bullard & Son Brewery 1868'.

9. Climb some steps and reach the remains of a hand pump in front of a decorated terracotta panel. This is Gilson's Conduit. The brewery was permitted to draw water from a well, on condition that a water point was provided for the public. Climb more steps to Westwick Street and turn left. After joining St Benedict's Street, go straight on at the traffic signal junction. Pass St Andrew's church on the right, and reach St George's Street on the left. Look left to see the large St Andrew's Hall, formerly the church of the Blackfriars Priory.

10. Do not follow the traffic route but go straight on along Princes Street, a narrow road. At the next junction, turn left down Elm Hill, passing the end of St Peter Hungate Church, now a museum. Swing right and pass a plane tree in the centre of a cobbled triangle. The tree replaced the large elm from which the hill derived its name.

Continue down the street. The houses on the left were merchants' houses, and were here in 1578. At the end of Elm Hill cross the road and turn right. Pass on the left the Maid's Head, an ancient coaching inn. Edward the Black Prince stayed here in the 14th century. Cross the road at the roundabout and you are in Tombland. Turn left through Erpingham Gate, back to the Cathedral.

PLACES OF INTEREST NEARBY

If you would like something different after all that history, at the University of East Anglia, on the edge of Norwich, is the *Sainsbury Arts Centre*. Housed in an imposing building by Sir Norman Foster, it holds a display of modern art with a major section illustrating world-wide ethnic art. Telephone: 01603 593199. Or what about a *river cruise*? Southern River Steamers run cruises along the rivers Wensum and Yare between May and September, and at Easter. Telephone: 01603 624051.

THE RIVER YARE AT SURLINGHAM

A walk through a lovely Broadland area, starting at Bramerton Common where there is a long staithe for Broads cruisers to berth. You walk beside the River Yare – one of Broadland's great rivers – and pass a secluded nature reserve, to come to the old Ferry House, before returning on a parallel route past a ruined church.

The Ferry House pub passed on the route

The Rivers Yare and Waveney comprise the main waterways in the southern part of the Norfolk Broads, flowing through a broad tidal estuary called Braydon Water, to the sea at Great Yarmouth. The River Yare reaches the very edge of Norwich where it ceases to be navigable, but ships sail up its tributary, the River Wensum, to the docks in Norwich. There was a pedestrian ferry across the river at Surlingham, but this is long since closed. The Ferry House still stands beside the staithe, serving the needs of Broads holidaymakers instead of the ferry users. The only crossing point of the River Yare today, in the 25 meandering miles between Great Yarmouth and Norwich, is the car ferry at Reedham.

Half way round this circular walk you pass the Ferry House, situated at the end of Ferry Road, Surlingham. Here you can relax in glorious surroundings, either at the bar or at riverside tables, sampling the varied fare on offer. This is a popular waterside pub serving people using the river. Telephone: 01508 538227.

- **HOW TO GET THERE:** Surlingham is a little village south-east of Norwich. From the A47 Norwich bypass, take the A146 towards Lowestoft. In less than ¼ mile, turn left at the first junction, towards Rockland St Mary. In 2 miles, at Kirby Bedon, turn left along a narrow road towards Woods End. Eventually follow the River Yare for about ¼ mile and just as the road climbs away from the river, reach Bramerton Common and the start of the walk.
- **PARKING:** There is a gravel lay-by at Bramerton Common. Should this spot be crowded, go on to Surlingham church, where there is room for a few cars. If parked at the church, you should follow the walk from paragraph 3 in the description.
- **LENGTH OF THE WALK:** 4 miles. Maps: OS Landranger sheet 134 Norwich and The Broads; OS Outdoor Leisure 40 The Broads (GR 295061).

THE WALK

1. Start by walking across Bramerton Common along the bank of the River Yare. At the far end of the mooring area, go right for a short distance and take a narrow path between a wooden fence on the left and a flint wall on the right. After going through a white gate, continue along a narrow footpath beside a bank which merges into a steep hill on the right. Steps lead up to dwellings here.

Another white gate leads to an open area where a broad stony track from the hill on the right gives access to a large riverside house. Go straight on, not along the track, but towards a pedestrian gate almost at the water's edge. Follow the narrow path beside the river. On the right is a magnificent garden and beyond it a fine house.

2. At the corner of the garden, go through another gate. At this point the public right of way divides. At low tide, when the water level in the river is low, you can continue along the riverbank. However, it is

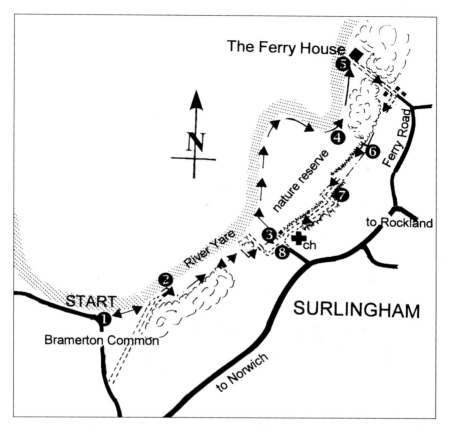

prudent to take a drier route, so turn right through a squeezer barrier and walk beside a hedge on the right. On reaching the corner of the field, go through a steel gate and turn left. The path lies at the foot of a wooded slope on the right. To the left, beyond a drainage ditch is a riverside field.

Pass a timber footbridge off to the left, which is the end of the riverbank path. Shortly after, enter the woods. Leave the wood and follow a barbed wire fence on the right, along the edge of a large field. You can glimpse the river on the left. Turn right at the corner of the field and climb away from the river, beside a wood on the left. Further up the hill swing left round the wood, passing a young plantation on the right. Come out to a surfaced drive and turn right for about 30 yards and then cross a stile on the left to follow a narrow footpath beside a wood on the left. The path bends right and later bends left.

3. Before long you reach Surlingham church. There is an interesting information board about Surlingham Church Marsh Nature Reserve here, which will enhance your enjoyment of the next part of the walk. From the church, with the churchyard wall on your right, follow the narrow grassy lane, passing an isolated flint cottage on the right. In about 250 yards the lane reaches sluices at the end of a drainage dyke. Continue beside the narrow reed-edged dyke on the left, with the marshes of the RSPB Nature Reserve on the right.

Eventually the path reaches the River Yare and you bend right to walk along the bank. The river is surprisingly wide here. Pass Ellis Hide, a bird hide overlooking the marshes and ponds on the right. Climb six steps to walk along higher ground, still beside the river. Soon descend more steps back to the original level. Pass a path off right which leads to another hide. Still keeping beside the river, come to a path to the right at the corner of the reserve.

4. Here go across a long timber bridge over a small backwater. Keep straight on along a narrow permissive footpath beside the river, and eventually, after crossing stiles, arrive at the Ferry House. There is a staithe on both sides of the river, but these days there is no ferry.

5. From the Ferry House, refreshed, leave the river along the access road with wooded marshy land on both sides. Reaching some houses at the edge of the marshes, turn right along a gravel drive, passing Willow Cottage on the right. Soon the drive becomes a grass path. Notice a fine house on the right and, close to the path, a dovecote on the roof of a garage. Cross a stile into a long meadow. Keep to the edge of the field with a wood on the right.

6. Turn right over a stile and then follow a path between a fence on the left and a hedge. A few yards on, ignore an inviting stile on the right which leads back to the river but keep straight on beside the hedge on the right. Before long cross a short marshy area on a board walk and continue along the path. Pass a Gun Club building and a cottage on the left. Squeeze past a gate and follow a grassy lane beside a reed-edged watercourse. The lane turns left and in about 100 yards you reach a junction of tracks.

7. Make a short diversion, turn left and very soon climb a few steps towards a ruined church. Just beyond the top of the steps and to the left of the path is a bronze plaque inscribed 'Ted Ellis 1909-1986 Naturalist'. This is the grave of a well-known local naturalist who lived and worked nearby and after whom the Ellis hide is named. Return to the track and continue straight on to Surlingham church.

8. The return to Bramerton is along the paths you used earlier. Therefore, turn right from the church and take the narrow footpath to the right of the drive to River Barn. On reaching the surfaced drive, turn right for about 30 yards and then go left along the footpath which eventually brings you back to the riverside. Skirt the fine garden and cross an open area to return through a white gate to Bramerton Common.

Places of Interest Nearby

Cross the River Yare on the tiny vehicle ferry at Reedham, an interesting experience in itself, to reach *Pettitts Animal Adventure Park*. Its attractions include rides, an adventure playground and animals. Telephone: 01493 701403.

Bramerton Common

GILLINGHAM:
THE RIVER WAVENEY FROM
BECCLES TO GELDESTON

Starting from Gillingham church, this lovely walk crosses the flood plain to Beccles Old Bridge, beckoned on by the commanding tower of St Michael's church. Then you join the bank of the River Waveney for a superb journey upstream to Geldeston Dyke, before returning to Gillingham along a minor road.

The river at Beccles

The River Waveney which forms the southern boundary of much of Norfolk is navigable to Geldeston Lock, about 2 miles west of Beccles. Beccles is a busy centre for the Broads, and walking beside the river you are likely to see cruisers and other craft. However, being near the limit of navigation, this part of the river is not so busy as other sections and you should find the walk quiet and peaceful. I saw a kingfisher here.

The walk passes the Wherry Inn at Geldeston, which is a comfortable and popular pub in the centre of the village. Blackboards in the bar display a short but varied menu. Their deep-fried Portuguese sardines served with mushrooms, tomatoes and French fries made an interesting and enjoyable meal. Other dishes include fresh prawns; gammon with pineapple or egg and a rack of pork with honey and garlic sauce. The tables outside make it a pleasant place to relax and take refreshment on a warm summer day. Telephone: 01508 518371.

- **HOW TO GET THERE:** The walk starts at Gillingham church a mile north-west of Beccles. Just south of the roundabout junction of the A146 with the A143, turn off north along a minor road (signed to the church).
- **PARKING:** Gillingham church is on a T-shaped cul-de-sac formed by the, now bypassed, old road and there is room for safe parking here. Alternatively, there is a good public car park close to the Quay in Beccles. Go to Beccles and follow the signs to the Quay. For any who park in Beccles, go to the Beccles Old Bridge, cross the river into Norfolk and follow the route description from paragraph 3.
- **LENGTH OF THE WALK:** 6 miles; a short cut reduces the distance to 4 miles. Maps: OS Landranger sheet 134 Norwich and The Broads; OS Outdoor Leisure 40 The Broads (GR 411922).

THE WALK

1. From Gillingham church go south (in the Beccles direction) to the end of the cul-de-sac and continue along a tarmac path, which leads to a footbridge over the main road. After joining an estate road, you soon reach a road into Gillingham.

2. Keep straight on past a road junction on the right. Soon pass the Swan public house and continue across the water meadows along a road called Gillingham Dam. Prominent on a hill in the distance is the tower of St Michael's church and around it, the lovely old town of Beccles. In about ½ mile you will come to Beccles Old Bridge over the River Waveney.

3. Do not cross the bridge but turn right down some steps at the end of the brick parapet and follow a stony track beside a concrete

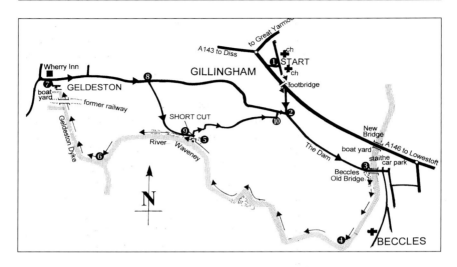

floodwall on the left. Keeping on the track, in about 250 yards cross a steel stile and follow the Broads Authority's green arrow waymark.

On reaching a small parking area at the end of the surfaced track, continue along a timber boardwalk beside the river where a number of craft are moored. On the left, beyond the river, private gardens with attractive lawns and flowerbeds sweep down to the riverbank. A gate at the end of the boardwalk leads to a grassy path, still beside the river. The path becomes narrower and climbs a small flood protection bank.

4. Follow the river, which gradually bends right. You are walking beside tall shrubs on the left but you can still catch glimpses of the adjacent river between the vegetation. Come to a wooden stile beside a steel gate and the path continues. Another stile leads into a more open area where cattle have grazed. A third stile and the footpath is narrower again.

5. Enter a wooded area and later come to a point where there is a small dock on the left and beyond it, a timber riverside building. Here the path is fenced on both sides. Continue along the path as it eventually bends left and joins a similar track at right angles. For a short cut, turn right and after crossing the route of the former railway, climb away from the river until you reach a road. Then continue from paragraph 9 below.

Continuing the main walk, turn left, back towards the tree-clad riverbank and continue beside the River Waveney. Now you are much closer to the river because there is no flood protection bank. Later, the path skirts round a large old boathouse and continues along the river bank.

6. When you come to a confluence of two wide rivers, the River Waveney bends sharp left while on the right is a waterway called Geldeston Dyke. At the junction is a large willow tree. Walk beside the Geldeston Dyke which, at first, is almost as wide as the Waveney but gets progressively narrower. Go under a former railway bridge on a path beside the Dyke. Should the waterside path be flooded or muddy, climb the railway embankment and descend the other side, which will bring you back to the path. Keep beside the water for 100 yards or so and, following the waymark, bend left round Rowan Craft boatyard and reach a gravel access drive. Turn right, leaving the boatyard by a gate and turn left along a minor road.

7. This is the village of Geldeston and very soon you reach a T-junction, opposite the Wherry Inn. Notice on the right, the old village hall with its Flemish gables. Turn right along the road.

8. Pass Geldeston Lodge on the left and take the first turning to the right, signed 'Dunburgh'.

9. In about ¼ mile come to a dwelling with wooden fencing, on the left, and on the right, a row of reflecting posts protecting a well tended grass verge. Those who have followed the short cut mentioned in paragraph 5, rejoin the route here, through a small green gate on the right. Keep along the road passing several dwellings.

10. After about ½ mile along a bendy minor road, and having entered Gillingham, make a sharp left bend to a T-junction. Turn right along The Street and then turn left to retrace your steps back to the start at the church.

PLACES OF INTEREST NEARBY
The Otter Trust has a large collection of otters together with a wide variety of wildfowl at its reserve in Earsham, close to the River Waveney. Light refreshments can be obtained at the Tea Room. Keep on the A143 to 1 mile west of Bungay. Telephone: 01986 893470.

BURGH CASTLE AND BREYDON WATER

There is so much to enjoy on this walk, starting from the church at Burgh Castle and following the river wall downstream for a view of Breydon Water. Then you return upstream to explore the Roman fort that once dominated this part of the then coastline, before an enjoyable walk back past working boatyards and staithes.

Breydon Water seen from the path

In defending this part of Britain from marauding hordes of invaders, from what is now Germany, the Romans built forts around the coast. One of these was at Burgh Castle, built around the year AD 280. It stands on the bank of the River Waveney at its confluence with the River Yare. Originally this site was on a wide inlet on the coast, but now the land has been built up over the passage of time and the River Yare flows out to the sea at Great Yarmouth.

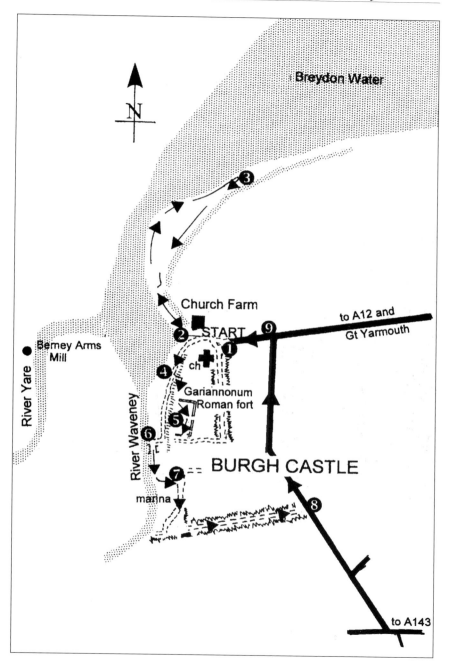

Between Burgh Castle and Great Yarmouth the river widens out to form Breydon Water, a shallow tidal estuary 3 miles long and ½ mile wide. Breydon Water, a Site of Special Scientific Interest, is an important nature reserve, where the receding tide reveals a large expanse of soft mud, which is a rich feeding ground for duck, geese and other wild fowl. The views and impressions of this area change completely with the states of the tide.

Built in 1788, Church Farm was converted to a pub in 1992. It still looks like a farm house! The restaurant has wide windows looking out over the rivers Waveney and Yare, and interesting artefacts decorate the walls including a cricket bat signed by England players, and a variety of old firearms. A popular pub, serving meals all day, the menu includes Barnsley chops, liver and bacon, and grilled gammon with two eggs. Vegetarian options include Marguinta (open mushrooms with ratatouille topped with cheese). There are many picnic tables outside and a children's play area. Telephone: 01493 780251.

- **HOW TO GET THERE:** Burgh Castle is about 3 miles west of the Gorleston area of Great Yarmouth. In the village, continue to the end of the road by the church.
- **PARKING:** There is space for one or two cars by the turning space at the end of the road by the church. In addition there is a gravel car park just inside the gate to Church Farm.
- **LENGTH OF THE WALK:** 3½ miles. Maps: OS Landranger sheet 134 Norwich and The Broads; OS Outdoor Leisure 40 The Broads (GR 476050).

THE WALK

1. From the end of the road, by the gateway to Church Farm, go through a kissing gate on a narrow lane down towards the river.

2. Keep straight on through a pair of wooden gates on to a new flood protection bank and walk beside the river on your left. Notice, on the opposite side of the water, the point where the River Waveney joins the River Yare. On the bank of the Yare is Berney Arms Mill, a tall isolated tower mill, formerly used for drainage. Continue along the bank passing through two more sets of gates.

3. Walk on a further 50 yards or so, drop down off the bank and make a U-turn. Now return through a meadow beside a broad ditch on the left. Climb back up the bank just beyond the middle set of gates, and continue back to the lane at the start of the flood protection wall. Turn right along a broad footpath between reed beds on the right and a wooded slope on the left.

4. In about 175 yards, look for and climb a flight of wooden stairs up the bank on the left. Walk beside the top of the slope and then climb more steps to the wall of the Roman fort Gariannonum.

5. Pass through into the fort area. Go half left and make your way to the entrance in the centre of the east wall. Here there is an information board about the site. When you are ready, cross to the centre of the south wall and go through a gap, making a slight descent to a footpath just beyond the wall and turn right.

6. On reaching the water's edge turn left over a bridge and continue along a path between fences. Just beyond The Fishermans Bar and shop, turn left beside the fence of Goodchild Marine boatyard.

Church Farm public house seen from across the water

7. At the road turn right and squeeze beside a steel barrier, following the Angles Way waymark along a surfaced track. There will probably be several large boats stored behind the fence on the right. Pass the Harbour Master's office on the left and the marina moorings on the right. At the corner of the moorings, where the surfaced track bends right, leave the track and swing left, pass a steel gate and continue along Porter's Loke, a lane between hedges.

8. Turn left at the road, and follow it, passing the entrances to several holiday sites.

9. In about ½ mile turn left at a T-junction back to the church.

PLACES OF INTEREST NEARBY

Great Yarmouth offers several attractions. Wander round the Town Walls, see the Old Merchant's House and explore The Rows, narrow lanes running between the Town Wall and the Quay. On the sea front is *The Butterfly Farm* where humming birds, tropical butterflies, terrapins and tropical fish are displayed. Telephone: 01493 842202.